COMPETITION MONOLOGUES

44 Contemporary Speeches from the Best Professionally Produced American Plays

Edited and with an Acting Introduction by
Roger Ellis

D1316964

UNIVERSITY
PRESS OF
AMERICA

Copyright © **1988** by

University Press of America,® Inc.

4720 Boston Way
Lanham, MD 20706

Library of Congress Cataloging-in-Publication Data

Competition monologues : 44 contemporary speeches from the best
professionally produced American plays / edited and with an
introduction by Roger Ellis.
p. cm.
Bibliography: p.
1. Monologues. 2. Acting—Auditions. 3. American drama—20th
century. I. Ellis, Roger, 1943–
PN2080.C64   1988
812'.045'08—dc 19   87–34632 CIP
ISBN 0–8191–6849–1 (alk. paper)
ISBN 0–8191–6850–5 (pbk. : alk. paper)

For Jeremy, Kady, and Zan

Acknowledgments

Among the many groups and individuals who have given me assistance over the years in compiling the material for this book and in seeing it through the publication process, there are several who deserve special thanks for their much needed efforts. The Research and Development Committee and the School of Communications at Grand Valley State College were instrumental in covering the costs of travel and in making arrangements with the authors for use of their material. All of the playwrights whose work is included here were very generous in granting me permission to use the extracts from their plays. Finally, I must also acknowledge the kindness of numerous agents who sent me scripts for perusal, and the efforts of many young actors whose performances helped me to select and to shape the monologues for inclusion.

C O N T E N T S

INTRODUCTION: To the Actor

Actors and Monologues

I've always felt that one of the worst burdens imposed on actors today is the demand that they audition with monologues. The monologue is now enshrined as part of the actor's standard equipment, just as essential as a resume, a union card, or an eight-by-ten glossy. Students must perform them for scholarship and entrance competitions, summer stock performers must run them by producers in thirty-to-sixty-second fragments at massive cattle calls, while other professionals must often deliver them to overworked and unsympathetic casting directors in offices or rehearsal halls or on unfamiliar theater stages.

Suddenly, that is, this administrative convenience of the dramatic monologue has become elevated to the status of the sink-or-swim entrance requirement (with devastating built-in judgments) for finding work in plays and often in the media. It is, after all, only an administrative convenience that directors use monologues at all. It would be totally unrealistic and impossible to expect every actor to bring along a friend for each audition in order to perform in a two-character scene. And so the monologue is used instead as a convenient device for looking closely at actors when casting plays.

But the problem is that every one of us--directors, actors, coaches, producers--frequently place too much weight upon this solo performance, or mistake its value in a casting situation. Actors, for example, often feel they must provide the character which is being sought (as if they're expected to read the auditors' minds); or they must "blow the auditors out of the room" with their monologues in order to get noticed; or they feel they should demonstrate as much "technique" as possible in the monologue so the director will know they're skilled and trained. On the other side of the table, casting people most frequently fall into the trap of expecting these kinds of monologue performances and of accepting them as final. Instead of looking for actors to develop a role, auditors tend to look for "type," for finished products. There is no time. The "right" person is out there. The pressure of the casting situation often prods directors and actors to rely overmuch upon the monologue as the main indicator of "who is the right character" to play the role.

All of these confusions--and more--muddy-up the waters of our casting situations, especially for actors. Not knowing exactly what the directors are looking for, even if you've read the script, you're left with a host of contradictory choices in selecting and performing your monologue. Here are a few that have always plagued me:

2

"Are they looking for the traditional character, the straight character? Do they want the correct interpretation of the speech at this particular moment of the play?"

"Can I get some inside information on what the directors <u>are</u> looking for in order to shape my performance better?"

"Are they looking for my <u>potential</u> as an actor, regardless of the monologue I choose? or the way I choose to interpret it?"

"Should I select a monologue from the play being cast? If I do, will I run up against the director's own idea of whom he wants for the part?"

"Will the directors be comparing me with the actors they've seen in this role before? or earlier today? Should I therefore use a totally-original monologue? or do something off-beat?"

"Do I need to score an impression with something bold and physical, or something dynamically written with strong emotions in order to earn a callback?"

"Does this monologue show a range of my abilities? Is it appropriate for the part (whatever it is)?"

It's almost as though you feel yourself part of some cookie-cutter process (mold-ville Hollywood gone berserk) frantically caught-up in the casting maze, trying to outguess the auditors as you decide which "character" they're looking for.

But alas! the monologue is here to stay and we all learn to live with it, and to deal with it as a feature of doing business in this business. Yet despite all this confusion about monologue auditions, there is a great deal that can be done to improve your performance of them in competitive situations. Monologue workshops are offered in many cities, and private coaching can be found wherever there are professional theatres. But there are few "handbooks" on the subject despite the fact that directors and coaches are pretty much in agreement on what goes into a good monologue audition. I'll be covering some of these points in the next few pages, but before we get into this, there is one fundamental thing I want to make clear: <u>a monologue can and should only demonstrate an actor's potential for a role</u>.

Yes, of course, the auditors are looking for the "right" actor to come along; but actors always make a big mistake by thinking the monologue can supply that magical pre-fabbed

"character" who will fill the director's bill. Never aim at
"character" in your monologue; aim at honest responses to the
dramatic situation. You can never know what exactly a director
will be seeking, or what will turn a director off. So it's
useless to try and it's a mistake to think of substituting a
posture, an attitude, or a character for the emotional truth
you've created and rehearsed. And, yes, there are always
directors who don't have the time to look carefully or who make
the mistake of trying to save themselves work. These lack the
confidence in their own abilities to coach an actor through
rehearsals in order for the character to develop. We must
suffer such people--in auditions and rehearsals--because they
give us work. But actors also make a mistake in trying to fit
themselves into this kind of a preconceived mold (which usually
rewards a director with an opening night performance hardly
different from the audition).

In these cases the actor has lost touch with the one thing
in the audition which can make his performance absolutely
unique, absolutely authentic: his own potential, himself. By
"going for the type" the actor is left only with a
simplification, a reduction, an abstract idea which is supposed
to fit the mold. In both cases the actor will find it
impossible to offer a real person, a person who responds fully
to the dramatic circumstances of the monologue because he is
delimited by the "type," by the expectations of somebody else.

The following suggestions for preparing monologues are all
based on this belief that a good monologue audition, like any
good acting performance, is never forgotten. Though you may not
be "right" for this particular play, you will certainly score a
strong impression in the auditors' memories. Producers and
directors have told me this many times, and they've also
stressed how quickly they can eliminate and forget actors who
are "acting all over the place" in monologue auditions, as
though "technique" or a "character" were theatrically
interesting. They are not, and I'm sure I'm not the only one
who's received calls months after I've been turned down for a
role--only to find later that the director remembered my acting
and called me back to read for another role he was casting
somewhere else.

For this reason I make my students in monologue classes
refer to themselves in the situation and not to the
"character." The temptation to throw up and hide behind a
character is always deadly. Actors must learn instead to embody
the character and experience the character's situation as fully
as possible. So in the suggestions which follow, remember
always to place yourself in the circumstances of the role and
avoid as much as possible distancing yourself from it,

4

intellectually or emotionally. Avoid analyzing or explaining your monologue in such terms as "My character is . . ." or "At this moment my character feels . . ." Always use yourself. As the great Stanislavski pointed out with regard to this "magic if" of acting: "Remove yourself from the plane of 'acting' and place yourself instead on the plane of your own human emotions."

Monologues, then, must at all times be a vehicle for revealing yourself, your responses in the character's situation. If the casting people are looking for a strong "type" you can never know just what that means to them; it's silly to worry about it because you'll either fit the type or you won't. What can and will interest them at all times is authentic, dynamic and impassioned acting; and a stereotype can never be as authentic as your own deeply-felt emotions.

So have enough confidence in yourself to respond with all the richness and truth of a human being's emotional and intellectual life to the dramatic problems that the monologue presents, instead of acting what you think the auditors want to see. Your personalization of the dramatic material will always reveal a more interesting and compelling actor that any lifeless "character type" is likely to produce. It's the necessary first step on the path which leads to a successful monologue audition.

Selecting Monologues

I've called this anthology "competition" monologues for the simple reason that all the pieces I've selected are specifically suited to the competitive situation of auditioning for plays and contests. This sets them apart from other monologue anthologies on the market which are little more than collections of long speeches taken from plays. Although these monologue books are frequently an actor's first step in finding material to use for auditions, it's important to remember that most of them are assembled by people who have no particular skill or experience in auditioning as actors, directors, or as coaches. Hence, they often lack those special features which distinguish speeches in plays from monologues that are well-suited to auditioning.

What are those special features? What are the drawbacks of monologues simply lifted from playscripts? One of them is the fact that a character in a play who speaks at length in a monologue may often simply be "talking to himself"--calmly going over some of the events in the plot or making observations about other characters. Also, many speeches with intense emotions usually occur at a point where the performance has already gained some momentum prior to the character's situation of finding himself or herself alone for a moment. Finally, many speeches you'll find in plays often discuss subjects which are nostalgic and reminiscent for the character.

None of these qualities will help you in an audition. A monologue aimed at commenting upon or advancing the plot of a play is likely to be useless and uninteresting to directors casting a different play. And even if those circumstances do yield a strong dramatic or emotional response in the speech, it often takes awhile to build up to it. In an audition situation you don't have the time to "work into" your piece, to build up emotional momentum as a play can do in performance. Your monologue must be strong and vital from the outset, since directors are usually only listening for the first fifteen seconds or so. And finally, nostalgic and reminiscent monologues simply lack the emotional energy you need to get onstage and perform a vital, compelling, and passionate audition. Most speeches taken verbatim from plays work well in the context of that play's production; but not all of them are specifically aimed at presenting a human being grappling with important problems, and in need of communicating that experience to someone else here and now. This is the main thing that makes a good audition piece.

The best monologues I've witnessed (acting abilities aside) have been those pieced-together from a two-person or three-person scene where the character is already involved in a strong give-and-take of ideas with others, struggling for communication and victory in getting what he or she wants. With the other character edited-out of the scene, the auditionee was able to patch together a single monologue from bits and pieces of dialogue. With this kind of material you give the auditors a chance to see a much wider range of your talent as you develop from beginning to end in the scene. You can then use the other character's lines as a springboard, as motivation for different reactions, different obstacles to encounter, new "events" which occur in the monologue and which force you to play constantly changing actions in response to them. I bring this up to stress the fact that there must always be other characters onstage with you, characters with whom you have a strong relationship as you deliver the speech to them.

Not all actors are competent playwrights, however. Editing together a series of shorter speeches into a single consistent situation with a beginning-middle-end is not easy to do. And writing your own monologue is always deadly (unless you're a playwright as competent as Shakespeare, Shaw, Lanford Wilson, Sam Shepard, and others). Nor are actors familiar with a wide range of recent scripts to choose from, especially scripts containing characters within the age range of young performers. Perhaps for this reason alone, monologue anthologies are handy, popular choices for actors seeking

6

auditioning material. But you will find that all the pieces included here possess that fundamental quality of a good monologue which I just mentioned: they aim at presenting a character grappling with problems which he or she considers vitally important, and who also feels a strong need to communicate that experience to someone else.

Some of these monologues have been taken intact from plays, others have been pieced together from a series of shorter speeches with the other characters edited-out. What is important, though, is that you concentrate upon that need to communicate in a relationship even though you're the only actor onstage at the audition. It is <u>relationship</u> which underlies every bit of acting you will ever do; and it must form the basis of single-character speeches just as it does in dramatic scenes with other characters.

Devising the Vis-a-vis

"Vis-a-vis" is a technical term for the other (imaginary) character to whom you're speaking. Michael Shurtleff, the widely-acclaimed auditions coach, recommends that you "bring a friend onstage with you so it won't seem so lonely" for you up there during your monologue. What he means is that you must have someone whom you're trying to <u>influence</u> during the monologue for it to work effectively. Without this other character "onstage" resisting you, attacking you, rejecting you, or even ignoring you, then your performance will tend to be much less energetic and focused.

Now it's not always possible to know who this listener actually is. Some of your monologues, of course, have probably been taken from plays where the listener(s) are fairly well-defined; for example, Katherine's famous speech at the close of The Taming of the Shrew where she is definitely speaking to the guests at the wedding party. But other plays may not be as familiar to you. The monologues in this book, for example, are all taken from recent plays which might be difficult, if not actually impossible for you to find and read.

It isn't necessary, however, to read the whole script in order to do an excellent monologue, any more than it's necessary to read the entire play to do a good cold reading. The script will, of course, always give you a better idea of the character; <u>but unless you're being asked to do a specific speech for the audition, then there is no reason to acquaint yourself with the whole play beforehand, and you should not feel at a disadvantage because of this.</u> You must instead become familiar with the given circumstances found in the monologue (a process of observation and deduction), and then add items from your own personal experience which are analogous to those of the character (a process of improvisation and substitution).

You'll find that all good monologues give some indication of who the listener is. As I discussed earlier, this should be a built-in feature of a good competition monologue: that it has a strong sense of struggle or conflict, and a strong need to communicate with someone. But these "given circumstances" are usually minimal, and in all cases they are not your own. They are those of the play, and like any acting performance, you must add your own personal belief to them in order to make them seem real, to give them life.

I don't want to discuss here the acting method called "substitution," whereby you substitute people, facts, emotions and the like from your own background for those of the play in order to identify with the role. Many techniques for accomplishing this--emotional memory, sensory recall, etc.--are well-known and described elsewhere. What I do want to stress, though, is whether you completely invent your vis-a-vis and the reasons why you're speaking to him or her, or whether you deduce it from the context of the monologue, what matters in either case is your commitment to the goal you're trying to accomplish in the speech, what you're trying to do to the other character. The casting people will never know what personal stimuli you're using to energize the speech; they'll only be concerned with the intensity and believability of your acting. And this is why the choice of a proper vis-a-vis can be enormously helpful to your monologue.

To begin with, you should pick an imaginary listener who is unsympathetic to your character's needs and desires. This will automatically ensure that there is conflict in the scene, and will force you to fight strongly for what you want. Stop for a moment and think of some of the most famous monologues and soliloquies ever written for actors by playwrights like Ben Jonson, Moliere, or Shakespeare. Conflict is always up front in their characters' long speeches. Although they appear to be alone, no character is every truly "alone" onstage. Hamlet, for example, is really talking "to" and "about" his father (who repeatedly whips Hamlet on to avenge his murder), his mother (who has cheapened herself by marrying Claudius), his stepfather-uncle (a murderer who has stolen Hamlet's inheritance), and his fiancee Ophelia (who insists on loving him despite his madness). His speeches are not pretty philosophical speculations for the audience's edification, but vital arguments--pro and con--about the need to take extreme action. Hamlet's soliloquies may be arguments "with himself" onstage, but they are also arguments with these other characters (many of whom he actually addresses in the lines of the speech). This is what makes them dramatic, exciting, and playable.

You must create this same kind of demanding vis-a-vis for yourself. Use someone from your own life because then you can see that person concretely in your imagination. Place him or her downstage of you (so you'll always be "open" to the directors), and visualize specific reactions of that person to all the important ideas in your monologue. Imagine him or her getting up to leave, shrugging the shoulders, about to voice a protest, open-mouthed in shock or disbelief at what you're saying. Use those reactions to reinforce your own delivery of the words, your changes in mood or approach, your different tactics to get that person to do what you want. Create a compelling relationship with your vis-a-vis and you'll add tremendous vitality to your monologue.

The other character should also be someone who is important to you, whose opinions and actions you need and respect. This person can be an enemy (Hamlet's Claudius is a "bloddy, bawdy, damnable villain"), or a friend or relation (Hamlet's Ophelia is someone he loves but whom he must reject and hurt). Frequently the best listeners are those, like Ophelia, with whom you have a love-hate relationship. This will always make your monologue performance more rich, mysterious, unpredictable and therefore interesting. No matter that your concerns aren't as politically weighty as those of Prince Hamlet, nor that your listeners aren't kings, queens, murderers and the like. All that matters in the audition is that you commit yourself absolutely to winning-over your vis-a-vis, just as Hamlet does in his situation.

If the stakes of this conflict are high enough for you, then your acting will automatically tend to become more vigorous and interesting to the casting people. The vis-a-vis should therefore be a character who is capable of providing whatever it is you need to turn your life around and win happiness. Your character's problem--your problem--is not something which can be overcome by mundane solutions which anyone can offer. Only this vis-a-vis can do it for you; only this dramatic encounter holds life or death importance for you. Which brings me to my next point: what is it you seek from your vis-a-vis?

Goals and Obstacles

It's often said that an ability to understand and to play goals and obstacles in a scene lies at the heart of good acting. An actor who knows--or who gives the audience the impression of knowing--what he or she wants in a scene, who speaks and acts purposefully, and who seems willing to engage in any conflict in order to achieve his or her purpose is an actor who will compel our attention and create a convincing character. Discovering or devising goals for your character is one-half the battle here; the other half is discovering or devising what it is about your vis-a-vis that prevents you from achieving it.

Your goal in the dramatic situation of the monologue is never single, it must always be multiple. In life we never get what we want without having to overcome many obstacles along the way: other drivers, ex-wives, domineering parents, unresponsive lovers, greedy bankers, and more. And in each encounter there will be a number of things we want from that other person. In fact, we often discover some of them only in the course of that encounter, _because_ of the encounter. Of course, this always happens in two-character scenes where the beats change as the scene develops; and remember that you're treating the monologue as a two-character scene during the audition. So in your speech you should look in the lines and in the context for what your character seeks and just what stands in his or her way. If it's not indicated in the text then you must invent and improvise your own. Then identify _how_ your goals change in the monologue as your character's thoughts develop.

These different goals must always be clear to you moment-by-moment. You must attack each of them strongly when they occur in the speech for effective variety, contrast, and pace. Uta Hagen points out that this is one of the most valuable things an actor can do in a monologue, playing that pattern of actions which will give dramatic shape and development to the speech. At the same time, your goals should change as the other characters--in this case, your vis-a-vis--_force_ you by their actions to change them. So use your vis-a-vis in two ways here: as a person from whom you _need_ something vital for your own happiness, and as a person who continually, in different ways, _denies_ you this victory. This will intensify the performance of your monologue by deepening the relationship between you; you will create and define that relationship by playing these patterns of goals and obstacles during the performance.

It is also important that you identify and phrase these goals in strong terms. Robert Cohen, a professional acting coach and director from southern California, recommends that actors use the idea of "winning a victory." This will help you to keep the stakes of the conflict important in your own mind. Aaron Frankel, a noted Broadway director uses the phrase "an itch that you've got to scratch." Michael Shurtleff calls it "what you'r fighting for" because the word "fight" is all-important for your energy and vitality during the audition. Jane Brody, a Shurtleff method teacher and the Director of

10

Chicago's Audition Centre, often uses the following terms in her workshops: "This is a scene about me in a love relationship with the other person. What is the problem we're having?"

I think the word "love" can be very useful in this respect, if you keep in mind that love means many things between people. The Romeo and Juliet kind of love is probably the most familiar to young actors, but it only describes one kind of relationship, and it is not all that common in plays, nor certainly in monologues. There is also the love of brother for sister, parent for child, wife for ex-husband, murderer for victim, friend for friend, therapist for patient, student for teacher, etc. Thus "love" means more than simply romantic affection; it can also signify respect, trust, support, friendship, dependency, comfort, cooperation, and other things. But by using the word "love" you automatically intensify and deepen the playing of all the feelings during the monologue audition.

Now very few dramatic scenes or monologues are written which deal with the happy fulfillment of one character's love for another. Even Romeo and Juliet, though their love is plainly very strong and pure, must overcome a host of obstacles in order to win the love they feel for each other: bickering parents, social disapproval, mocking friends, and even scheduling problems which arise from finding suitable times and places for their lovemaking. They are continually involved with planning secretly, resisting their parents, persuading Friar Lawrence, escaping jail, etc. In most plays it is the denial of love, from a variety of sources, which propels the action forward.

You must identify in your monologue what kind of love your character is seeking, and what denials he or she is encountering. You vis-a-vis is the only person who can help you towards these goals, and you need that person here and now. Try to be very concrete about what you want your vis-a-vis to do, and what you are trying to do to that character at each and every moment in the scene. Some workable choices in this respect might be "to manipulate." "to abuse," "to cause guilt," "to seduce," "to blame," "to get even," "to flatter," and so on. Reinforce these with two or three concrete physical activities for you to perform onstage during the audition. And always remember that the casting directors will never know what these goals actually are; they'll only be attentive to the force of your acting, to the energy with which you play the monologue's dramatic situation.

Getting Onstage

One final point, critical for an audition, needs to be

mentioned here. <u>Remember that acting in an audition will always</u> <u>differ from acting in a play or in a studio scene in that the</u> <u>audition performance requires vitality right from the outset.</u> You must compel the director's attention, curiosity, and interest during the first few moments. Directors usually make crucial decisions about your abilities from the way you take the stage and introduce yourself to them, even before you begin "acting." A cliche that is nonetheless true is that directors often reach a decision about you in the first fifteen seconds of your audition.

Most of the monologues I've selected for this anthology provide good strong acting choices from the outset of the speech, and you must remember to play these strongly. Again, some monologues can give clear indications of such choices in the lines themselves; others require that <u>you</u> build-in your own circumstances, the importance of this dramatic encounter, not only throughout the speech but especially at the beginning.

I can't say too much about this need to kick-off your audition with energy and drive. Most actors already know that you must "get your best up front" and "lead with your strengths" either on a resume or in the audition. And many actors have their own methods for doing this in performance. Sometimes (rarely, I think) the motivation for attacking strongly from the outset is built into the speech itself, or in the given circumstances of the play. Obviously in the performance of a whole play this sort of motivation is part of the actor's consistent "through-line;" but in an audition you don't have this emotional momentum to bank upon. You simply make your entrance, do your introduction to the auditors, then--bang!-- you're on.

I think you need more than just the given circumstances of the play or the monologue itself in order to accomplish this effectively. No matter how compelling your character's situation may be in dramatic terms, those terms are not your own--they are the play's. What <u>you</u> need as an actor is something else, some personal trigger for your emotional commitment and belief which can propel you into the first moments of the monologue with little or no preparation.

Actors do this most frequently by using Stanislavski's approach called "emotional memory." All of us have a wealth of intense emotional experience in our past lives. Often we repress such knowledge because it's painful: memories of death and loss, the breakup of a love relationship, an accident which occurred to you or to a loved one. On the other hand, we frequently do call to mind or "conjure up" the intense <u>positive</u> memories and feelings from our past. Is there anyone who hasn't daydreamed or "replayed scenarios" of those happy times in order to imaginatively re-live them? Moments of victory in a ballgame, the thrill and tingle of that first kiss with someone special, the surprise and delight in receiving a long-awaited message or gift? Often we cherish such experiences in our waking fantasies for years after they originally occurred; and invariably they carry along with them many related <u>sensory</u> impressions: the fragrance of perfume, the chill of the air, the colors of the setting, and so on. <u>These</u> are the kinds of vivid images you need to energize the monologue from the opening moment.

You can evoke these strong feelings in yourself very easily by finding a key word or image which serves as an instant trigger for recalling the experience. In everyday life, isn't this how it frequently happens? The sound of a familiar tune, a casual remark by someone, the discovery of some long-forgotten object in an old box--and suddenly we're plunged into the sadness or the fear or the ecstasy of remembrance. Indeed, it's often more intense in recollection (or so it seems) than it was at the time. Actors do this frequently in order to cry onstage, to register shock or joy or fear.

So once you've rehearsed other aspects of your monologues, look to add this kind of inciting action at the opening in order "to be on" from the very first. An unmistakable kiss of death in any audition is an actor taking forever to "get into character" before beginning, while the directors lose interest and curiosity with each dismal second that passes. And then to have the same person slowly drift into the piece as he or she works into the heart of the speech. By that time, of course, the auditors are usually sending out for more coffee, leafing through their notes of prior auditionees, or fumbling under their seats for a dropped pencil. They let you continue, perhaps, out of courtesy or because something might eventually "happen" as you drone on in the background. But most of the time you're only just digging yourself out of the grave you created in the opening moments.

Most people who don't understand acting at all hold very different ideas about how their own emotions operate. They don't believe that emotion can--or even should--be turned on-and-off like a faucet because there's something arbitrary, dishonest, or phony about that when they do it in real life. As an actor, though, you're automatically more in touch with and more in control of your emotional life than ordinary people. You understand that the emotional "truth" of a dramatic situation can be communicated and expressed to an audience by many methods--and often without your actually "feeling" anything during the performance (except perhaps for stage fright!). I'm often amazed after a performance when a spectator tells me that some moment was "so moving and believable" when in fact I was totally unmoved onstage at the time it happened; or when I <u>was</u> acting my guts out and the same person says that it wasn't believable or it seemed false. Ah, the tricks and techniques we use in this business to create lies like truth!

So with this final suggestion to energize the opening moments of your monologue, look for those personal associations and key words or images that can trigger the strong emotional commitment you need to get out onstage with focus and purposefulness. It's useful and necessary in <u>every</u> audition. And who knows? If your emotional memory contains an incident analogous or even identical to that of your character, then so much the better. It sometimes happens.

Good luck with the monologues which follow. And keep in mind that the prefatory remarks at the head of each are only <u>suggestions</u> for you. They're simply things to consider, handy departure points for the unique choices <u>you</u> should add in order to create a vital, compelling human relationship onstage.

NOTES ON THE MONOLOGUES

1. All the monologues can be performed within a two-minute time limit, and many are as short as one minute. Shorter selections should be developed by editing-out material <u>internally</u>, rather than by simply chopping-off the beginning or ending lines.

2. Where the monologue <u>specifically</u> requires an actor of a particular ethnic background, this has been indicated. Many of the monologues, however, are suitable for performers of any ethnic background whatsoever.

3. The age range of the character indicated at the top of each selection is only a rough suggestion. The age of any dramatic character is not necessarily the same as the performer's actual age, since "range" means what an actor is physically and emotionally capable of playing. You should therefore use your own judgment in deciding upon the actual age of the character, and whether the piece falls within your range.

4. The designations "comic/serious/seriocomic" are also suggestions and you should not feel absolutely constrained to adhere to these guidelines.

5. The terms "ladder-type" and "stepping-stone" monologue are occasionally used in the prefatory notes. A ladder-type

14

speech is one which builds in emotional intensity more-or-less consistently from beginning to end (sometimes called a "climactic" speech). The stepping-stone monologue creates emotional peaks at various points, according to various stimuli during the speech. Its "high point" may sometimes occur at the end, but it cannot be effectively played as a "simple," gradual build in intensity.

MONOLOGUES FOR MEN

Buck by Ronald Ribman

Buck - 20's   Male - Serious

In this difficult monologue the actor must work at developing genuinely honest feelings towards the pain of being separated from his child, his feelings of resentment and victimization, and his fear of becoming anonymous and unimportant in his child's life. Above all the actor must resist the temptation to play the character as a "loser" which is always theatrically unexciting; and instead play "to win" which is a more theatrically compelling choice.

They got me back in the playground again, Charlie. The same cruddy playground across the street from the apartment I spent five years of my life in with Kenny . . . first rocking him in the carriage, then watching him walk, holding on to my fingers, then one day just going off by himself. And I can see the two of them standing on the terrace, staring down at me through those rotting ficus bushes he planted. And when the reconaissance is finished with, they move inside for the discussion: "Should we send the kid out, or risk another battle over visitation privileges?" You know how many times I've been to court with them since the divorce? Four times. Four times! And I always win because we always get the same judge. She issues order after order demanding that I be allowed to see my son. The only problem is that it never does any good. My wife has a special dispensation from God to throw my court orders into the garbage can while I have to obey hers down to the letter of the law. "If you don't have him back in four hours, I'll get a court order!" And by God, she will. I'm

17

scared, Charlie. I'm so scared. Scared that they're not going to bring him out to me, scared that if I can't keep up my support payments they'll keep him away from me for good, scared that no matter what I do I'm gonna lose him anyway.

The Incredibly famous Willy Rivers by Stephen Metcalfe

Prisoner - 20's   Male - Serious

This monologue allows a wide range of vivid character choices on the actor's part. The sociopath is speaking to his victim who escaped alive, though crippled. A sense of guilt or remorse is nowhere evident. In this stepping-stone type of monologue, the prisoner's delusions of power and self-importance permit the young actor to develop numerous personal substitutions from current events in his own experience, in order to bring the situation home in realistic detail.

You ever killed anybody? Ever want to? I bet you have. It's great. You're so in control. Of course I'm talking premeditated. You're so . . . powerful. You walk down the street and no one knows how powerful you are. You're like God. All you have to do is act and everything changes. You've taken a color out of a painting and substituted one of your own. You've given somebody else's melody different notes. You're a pebble that's been dropped in a pond. Concentric circles get wider and wider. When you're capable of killing, you're not afraid of anyone! You laugh inside 'cause you know that hardly anybody is capable of striking out the way you are. For keeps. If you must know, it was nothing personal. When I pulled the trigger I wasn't even thinking of you. No. I was thinking of me. I was thinking of me and what everybody

18

else was gonna be thinking of me. They were gonna and that's something. I'm a pretty far-out dude, you know.

Candide, or Optimism by Len Jenkin

Don Fernando - 30's   Male - Serious

This ladder-type monologue requires sharp characterization from the very outset. Physical details in gesture and movement are especially important and challenging, but technique must not stifle the character's underlying passionate hatred of his enemies which propels the speech. The monologue reaches a strong climax at the very end. The situation is rich with emotional colors of self-adulation, sarcasm, and arrogance which may be strongly established as the monologue develops.

I take care of my people, General Candide, in the spheres. The religious sphere, the political sphere, and of course, the sphere of fashion. Many of the people of Paraguay have affected my particular curve of moustache, since I was called to office. In fact, artificial ones are being sold in the shops. You can't know what a pleasure it is, what an example of your people's devotion, to see your moustache passing you by, on the Boulevard des Maricons. I know this must sound strange to someone from the sophisticated land of Westphalia, but my people are like children. You would not believe their naivete. You'd laugh yourself sick at some of their beliefs. They believe, for example, that this is the best of all possible worlds and that Paraguay is the finest nation in it--this fetid swamp that I am struggling to bring into the modern world, so that we can have a meaningful congress with the capitols of Europe. The revolution never ends. It is always necessary to stamp out revisionist elements, rising up in the faithful population like maggots in dead sheep. Despite enlightened government practices, some of my people have been seduced by these Jesuits. Their ludicrous Holy Commandante tells tham that the Paraguay we all love is just a dream in my head. That as soon as they kill me, the cities will dissolve, the jungle will dissolve, and the primal ooze will return. This Holy Commandante of the Jesuits is treated like a God. KILL HIM!

Principia Scriptoriae by **Richard Nelson**

Ernesto - 20's   Hispanic Male - Seriocomic

This monologue is patched-together from a two-character scene, and you should look to add reactions from the vis-a-vis in order to motivate the changing reactions of Ernesto. He is a man feeling somewhat out of place in England, as the monologue explains. The speech is rich in reactions and changes of mood as Ernesto describes one aspect of his experience overseas studying at a famous university.

You know, it's not at all like everyone says it is--Cambridge, Bill, English universities in general, actually. Oxbridge, I mean. They're not all homosexual. Everyone said they were-- before I left. Everyone who talked to my mother did. You wouldn't believe the bizarre conversations my mother and I had before I left. It's not often that a son gets such a clear picture of just how his mother's mind works. There is a good reason for that. There is a humane reason for that. Here is this nice upper-middle-class lady--and what does she start to do: take her only son around to brothels. Mind you, the better brothels, but still. I'm not saying she went in. God forbid.

20

She just took me around. She stayed outside. She just hung around outside. And paid. This is true. There can be some really strange shit down here. People can be really fucked up down here. She'd pay and stay outside. But first they'd have to haggle, though. I'm standing there and they are haggling over the price. My mother and the prostitute. That sort of does something to one's sense of pride. And none of it would have happened if the priest hadn't told her about English universities. The ideas people get into their heads.

The Incredibly Famous Willy Rivers, by Stephen Metcalfe

Willy - late 20's   Male - Serious

This facinating monologue is spoken by an intended murder victim to his assailant. The attack has ruined Willy's career, as he explains, because of the injuries he sustained. Yet despite the apparent seriousness and bitterness in the situation, there is still opportunity for humor and discoveries as the piece develops.

I want to thank you. You coulda gone after a really big, big name but did you? No! You chose me! You are the straw that has stirred my drink! And talk about personal enlightenment! The things I was concerned with, man! I wasn't concerned with the things that most people are concerned with. Breakfast, lunch, dinner. No, not me. I was in search of meaningful existence. Thanks to you, now I'm barely into surviving. It makes living risky. It makes it intriguing on a daily basis. Nothing like facing death to make existence meaningful, right?

21

No! I don't blame you, really, it was my mistake. I spent all my time trying to be famous. I might as well have painted a bull's-eye on my back. A low profile, that's the ticket. Keep your head down and out of the line of fire. Those who know, buddy, those who really control, those who play the pieces, the chessmasters, buddy, the suits, they're faceless. They're smart. I wasn't smart at all. My priorities got all fucked up. Creative, special, famous. Bullshit! When a person becomes famous for something as senseless as pulling a trigger, why try to be famous at all.

Crossing Niagara, by Alonso Alegria

Blondin - late 20's   Male - Serious

This monologue requires good ability to sustain interest in a stepping-stone type of speech. The compelling quality of Blondin's dream propels the narrative; and the actor's ability to see and create for the auditors the vivid details of that dream is essential for it to work in performance.

"The great Blondin, his hands burnt by the tightrope, arrived back at the American anchor point after having slipp--" They print those lies to sell more newspapers. I'd checked everything before going on, but all of a sudden I'm on a swing two hundred feet high, I'm like the end of a pendulum! I'm a tightrope walker, not a human monkey! The most amazing thing about that incident was arriving back at the anchor point. They fell silent and stood away from me when I collapsed on the ground, half-dead. Later I found out something I'll never

22

forget.   While I was hanging for my life onto that rope,

everybody started betting I would survive.   Astronomical odds,

fifty-to-one, a hundred-to-one!   Can you believe that?   I was

very moved by that.   Of course when I was the great Blondin,

high and mighty on my rope, people bet thousands on my death.

It seems that when you see that someone is about to die, you

never bet on the side of death.   If you're going to bet, you bet

on his surviving.   Things like this--they happen so seldom they

surprise you.

End of the World by Arthur Kopit

Trent - 28   Male - Serious

This monologue is spoken by a playwright struggling to make
sense of an issue about which he's been commissioned to write a
play.   His vis-a-vis is the man who has given him the
commission.   The piece contains occasional moments of black
humor, as well as touching moments of sadness, personal
helplessness, and near emotional breakdown.   It also contains a
strong climax which must be clearly motivated by the intensity
of feeling which underlies the speech from the beginning.

I cannot write a play from this material, NO one can write a

play from this material!   This stuff is INDESCRIBABLE.   Look,

there are certain things playwrights know!   One of those is what

makes a play.   This material does not!   In every play there is a

central character and this central character does not just want

something; he NEEDS something, needs it so badly that if he

doesn't get this thing he will die . . . not necessarily

physically, could be emotionally, spiritually, all right?   In fact, dramatically, the worse his potential fate, the better. But! BUT! Only up to a point. And that's the problem in this instance. Here the consequences of failure are so far beyond our imagination, so far beyond anything we have every experienced, or even <u>DREAMED</u>, an audience could not believe, fully believe, what it was watching . . . I cannot READ this stuff anymore! I DON'T WANT TO <u>READ</u> ABOUT THIS STUFF ANYMORE! "The Prompt and Delayed Effects of Thermonuclear Explosions" is not what I wish to read at night! I am scaring the shit out of my family! My son runs from me in HORROR when he sees me coming. You know why? Because I have become a sentimental goddam dishrag! I see him walking toward me and I start to weep. I see him playing on the lawn with his dogs and I start to weep. I DON'T WANT TO HAVE TO THINK ABOUT THIS STUFF EVERY DAY! WHAT SORT OF PEOPLE CAN <u>THINK ABOUT THIS EVERY DAY</u>?

<u>Angels Fall</u>, by Lanford Wilson

Zap - 20's   Hispanic Male - Seriocomic

<u>This monologue contains strong, vivid description in the narrative sections, as well as an energetic and positive climax at the very end. The actor should rehearse to enjoy and involve himself in the enthusiastic description of an early memory which has colored and inspired his whole life as a tennis pro. Then towards the end look to spell-out the philosophical conclusion which the character draws from his experience. The elements of importance and discovery should be everywhere present.</u>

Like when I found out I was a tennis player. I said my novenas, man. It was really weird. I was like in the fifth grade and I was watching these two hamburgers on some practice court, and

24

one of them hands me his racket. So I threw up a toss like I'd seen them do and zap! Three inches over the net, two inches inside the line. There wasn't nobody over there, but that was an ace, man. You should have heard those guys razz me. I mean, they was really on my case. And I think that's the first time anybody ever looked at me. I mean, I was skinny, you've never seen--most of the girls in my homeroom had about twenty pounds on me. So this guy shows me a backhand! Right down the line. And the thing is, that's where I wanted it. I saw the ball come at me, and I said I'm gonna backhand this sucker right down the line, and I did. So then they took their ball back. Which I don't blame them, 'cause no high school hotshot is gonna get off on being showed up by this eleven year-old creep that's built like a parking meter, you know? But that was it. I hit that first ball and I said, "This is me. This is what I do. What I do is tennis."

Les Blancs by Lorraine Hansberry

Tshembe - 20's   Black Male - Serious

This is a stepping-stone type of monologue which challenges the actor to sustain a strong note of underlying intensity from the very outset. The performer must not allow Tshembe's thoughts to ramble, but must instead develop definite emotional attitudes towards the conditions he describes: bitterness, sarcasm, complaint, contempt, and occasionally humor. The choice of an unsympathetic vis-a-vis can be especially helpful as the speech develops.

What has he done in Europe? Talk! Talk, talk, talk. That is what the African does in Europe. He wanders around in the cold in his thin suits and he <u>talks</u>. There is a great deal of pomp. In Europe the European is--very civilized. When our delegations are ushered in, and our people have said what they came to say, the Europeans have a way of looking hurt as if they have never heard of these things before. And presently we sit there feeling almost as if it is we who have been unreasonable. And then they stand up--it is always the Europeans who stand up first--and they say: Well. There are undoubtedly some valid things in what you have had to say . . . but we musn't forget, must we, there are valid things in what the settlers say? Therefore, we will write a report, which will be forwarded to the Foreign Secretary, who will forward it to the Prime Minister, who will approve it for forwarding to the settler government in Zatembe--who will laugh and not even read it. <u>That</u> is what Kumalo has been doing in Europe. <u>That</u> is what he will do in Zatembe.

Love's Labours Wonne, by Don Nigro

Shakespeare - 28   Male - Serious

This monologue creates a strong mood and reveals some of Shakespeare's dark, manic genius in powerful flashes. The actor must be especially careful of the pacing and avoid self-indulgence because the character's thoughts erupt unpredictably. The performer can also use the audition space to good advantage since the monologue specifically refers to locations on a theatrical stage in the first section. Finally, the piece offers the actor a wide range of unique choices for strong emotional attitudes towards the theatre, its audiences, and the auditors themselves.

When I was young I dreamed of this. The Globe's a little world of looking glass in which I see dark fantasies of violence and lechery played out for me. Up in the loft, the pigeon-haunted heaven peopled mostly by musicians, an unrealistic touch. The boards on which I walk are earth and do have worms. Verisimilitude. Down the spidered trap is hell, it's cold, but lovely rats. A tidy Christian world in which to smear myself with pagan metaphor and play out mindless rituals. But safe. I've built a universe of lies, all this is nothing. I am terrified of nothing, why won't my hand stop shaking? When the gun misfired in Tamburlaine and killed the pregnant woman in the audience, now there was theatre! There was a working metaphor, something done. I hate you people. Cannibals. God eats the children of my flesh, you eat the children of my soul. This place is dressed in lies and made of death, the substance of this place is death. I rot and rot and thereby hangs the tale.

Souvenirs, by Sheldon Rosen

Peter - 28   Black Male - Serious

In this monologue Peter speaks feelingly of his island culture to a white man whom he knows will never understand him. He is warning his vis-a-vis of immanent danger in this foreign place. The speech should be played with strong irony, mystery and secrecy. It can also tolerate an occasional note of humor. All this is difficult to achieve without allowing the intensity to sag. The humor is subtle, and this too is a challenge to play.

It is everybody's cause! Everything is connected, don't you know that? Just like the wave that comes here to the shore is connected to the wave out there in the ocean thousands of miles

27

away. I know that as a fact. What we burn here is carried in the wind to your soil. What is murdered here will haunt your lives the same way! There is someone you should meet. My friend, Medwin. It was his idea that I talk to you. Medwin will be able to convince you. He taught me that to care about other people was not only good, it was smart. He said not caring was a disease that was sweeping the world and that there would be so much not caring going on that the earth itself would stop caring one day and wouldn't turn around the sun any longer. Medwin, he's going to be the savior of this island.

Los Vendidos, by Luis M. Valdez

Sancho - 20's   Chicano male - Comic

In this play, one of Valdez' funniest creations for the San Francisco Mime Troupe, the character Sancho mimics the gringo's materialistic approach to every aspect of his society, including the migrant farm workers. Numerous personal substitutions for the vis-a-vis can be made in this well-paced monologue; and its hard-sell tone makes it strongly outer-directed.

Well, you come to the right place, lady. This is Honest Sancho's Used Mexican lot, and we got all types here. Step right over here to the center of the shop, lady. This is our standard farm work model. As you can see, in the words of our beloved Senator George Murphy, he is "built close to the ground." Also take special notice of his four-ply Goodyear huaraches, made from the rain tire. This wide-brimmed sombrero is an extra added feature--keeps off the sun, rain, and dust. And our farmworker model is friendly. Muy amable. Loves his

28

patrones! But his most attractive feature is that he's hard-working. Do you see those little holes on his arms that appear to be pores? During those hot sluggish days in the field, when the vines or the branches get so entangled, it's almost impossible to move; these holes emit a certain grease that allows our model to slip and slide right through the crop with no trouble at all. Senorita, you are looking at the Volkswagen of Mexicans. Pennies a day is all it takes. One plate of beans and tortillas will keep him going all day. That, and chile. Plenty of chile. Chile jalapenos, chili verde, chile colorado. You know these new farm labor camps our Honorable Governor Reagan has built out by Parlier or Raisin City? They were designed with our model in mind. Five, six, seven, even ten in one of those shacks will give you no trouble at all. You can even leave him out in the field overnight with no worry!

Final Passages, by Robert Shenkkan

Tom--20's   Male - Serious

This monologue challenges the actor to create a strong sense of mood as he recalls and becomes sucked-up into the nightmare of helplessly witnessing a tragedy taking place. The actor must not fall into the trap of allowing the character's memories to dampen the performance energy. Very careful attention to pace is therefore important, as well as the character's need to win understanding from his vis-a-vis. The short and choppy sentence structure must be used energetically to reveal the character's fears and desperate need to sort-out and articulate his tangled emotions.

When I was ten I watched a loose team of horses trample a little girl to death. Hot, bright day. Sun so sharp it'd peel your

29

scalp back like a razor. No wind. Air heavy. Breath hard.
I'm sittin' on the sidewalk. Back pressed hard into a brick
wall. Tryin' to wrap a little shadow over me. Sweat gluin' my
shirt to the brick. Nine, ten feet from me, there's a little
brown girl in the mud. Buildin' little mounds, then laughin',
squealin' as she kicks 'em to pieces. Across the street, old
man rearrangin' the fruit outside his store. Peels an orange.
Eats it. I watch the juice drop down his chin. Little girl's
mother leans out a window. Yells at her to come in. Little
girl ignores her. I feel it first. Runnin' up my spine. The
sidewalk start to shake, hums like a sheet about to snap. Then
I hear it. Real low at first. A crazy poundin', yellin'. Then
they're there. Right there. Roundin' the corner. A team of
four big dray horses, lashed to an empty wagon. Spooked,
runnin' scared. Manes whippin' back. All hoofs and wild eyes
and spit. Throwin' up the ground behind 'em like a black
cloud. We all watchin': me, the old man, the woman at the
window, the little girl. Everythin' just stops. Still.
Stops. Nobody moves. Nobody yells. And then they're past.
Racin' down the street. Out of sight. Just a faint rumble.
Then nothin'. Just quiet. Nothin'. The little girl is gone.
Complete gone. Like she's never been there. The woman at the
window starts to cry. I hear flies. Even when I knew, I
couldn't stop it. Couldn't stop things. Like those horses . . .
like what I did. Couldn't stop it. Couldn't stop it.

End of the World, by Arthur Kopit

Berent - 28   Male - Comic

This black comic monologue is spoken by a character desperately trying to make sense of an issue he feels absolutely compelled to justify, yet which defies any rational explanation. The character is struggling throughout to arrange all the pieces of the puzzle in a meaningful way, and the manic quality of that struggle frequently becomes quite comic. It is not so much a situation of the character trying to convince his vis-a-vis as it is of the character trying to convince himself at the same time. Discovery and game-playing thus become major comic elements in the performance.

What we must do--very simple: we must stop regarding nuclear war as some kind of goddam inevitable holocaust . . . and start looking at it as a goddam WAR! We have to learn how to wage nuclear war _rationally_. You see, even though a strong case can be made for the fact that nuclear war is essentially an act of insane desperation, and therefore fundamentally irrational, this doesn't mean that once you're in the thing you shouldn't do it _right!_ _Limited_ nuclear war. No one can win an all-out nuclear war. Unless, of course, the other side decides not to hit back, and one could never count on that, ALTHOUGH, I must say, in all the scenarios I've seen, the side that hits first definitely comes out best. So if push comes to shove, you do go first, no question of it, particularly if you employ what we call a controlled counterforce strike with restraint. In effect, you hit everything but your opponent's cities. His cities are held hostage. And what you do is, you tell him you'll demolish them if he doesn't capitulate. Now, this is actually quite

31

reasonable, _if_, big if, _big_ if, IF you have an adequate civil-defence system. That way, even if the Russians strike back, you should be able to absorb the blow and still have enough left to strike back at _them_. And this time just wipe them out. This is what I mean when I talk about credibility. What I have just described to you is a CREDIBLE offensive and defensive nuclear strategy. What we have now, forgive my French, is diddly-shit.

_K-2_, by Patrick Meyers

Taylor - 28   Male - Serious

In this bitterly ironic speech the actor must look for a variety of emotional choices to counterpoint the dominant note of anger. It can begin with a very aggressive attack, but the major climax is reserved until the very end, which means that the actor must carefully pattern the development throughout. Its strong points are a clear vis-a-vis, vivid diction, and powerful urgency in the dramatic situation.

Listen, Harold, you don't know what's goin' on down there all around you every day, every night--while you sleep, make love with Cindy, eat Chinese food, play with atoms at Lawrence Radiation Center. All around you all the time, you don't know, buddy. Christ, if you guys had any idea of what's really goin' on out there under your fuckin' noses, you'd be so damned scared you'd shit and die. There's a war goin' on down there--and the barbarians are winning! They're kickin' our civilized asses all over the streets. You know that out of every ten faces I prosecute--one is white, two are brown, and the other seven are black? What does that tell you Harold? Let me tell you what

32

your God damn bigger and better free lunch has produced. It's produced a black male, average age thirteen to twenty-five, who weighs between one-hundred and thirty and two-hundred and twenty pounds, who has the reflexes of a rattler, the strength of a rhino, and the compassion of a pit bull. He can rip off you and your grandma before you can count to one and he'll take it all-- your money, your clothes, your assholes--both of 'em--and he'll get her false teeth! That's what you get when you take away somebody's dignity and try to make it up to 'em by givin' 'em a free bag of groceries and a place to sleep. And I put 'em away every day. I make sure they get their three squares and a place to flop--behind fifty foot walls with some gun towers up top. That's what you pay me to do, Harold, and I do it extremely well. I do it to clean up after all you polyanna jerks. I do it for you and Cindy, Harold. I do it "to protect and serve" what little of our society is left.

The Grunt Childe, by Lawrence O'Sullivan

Drummond - 20's - 30's   Male - Serious

This monologue contains strong feelings of bitterness and anger from the very beginning through the final climax. Those emotions, however, need to be counterpointed here and there by Drummond's sense of helplessness, by his alienation from a civilian society which will never understand the reality that is Vietnam, and by his underlying sadness over the hopeless suffering he has witnessed. The actor should resist the temptation to play the speech glibly from an attitude of righteous indignation, and instead reveal a character struggling to find the right words to describe a situation which is indescribable.

What the hell are those cameras doing in my theatre of war? What the hell is this TV studio doing in the middle of Saigon? What's so major about a couple of reporters getting zapped over here, Senator? What the hell do you people think Vietnam is, a motion picture location where you can film John Wayne killing all the bad guys with one hand while handing out Hershey bars and Juicy Fruit gum with the other? This is a theatre of war, goddam it! It's a live performance of murder and madness that's been going on since Cain knocked the shit out of Abel and you all know it. That's why you can't sleep nights, Miller, you came to the wrong theatre and witnessed a performance that'll be a rerun of the nightmarish memories of your mind every time you turn out the lights. Do you cry out at night? I may not agree with what you've done but it took guts and I admire people with guts, that's why I'm here, to speak up for you and all the rest of us who'll have to go home and burn our uniforms because of these, these "atrocities?" You call that an "atrocity?" Where were you at Hiroshima? Christ, there were nothing but women and children. And probably some old men and a couple of goats too. That was your war, wasn't it, Senator? You all went home heroes. Well, I wonder what your welcome would have been if Mr. Reporter and his TV cameras had been there to serve up the sight of those blistered and burned bodies to the American public along with their TV dinners. No! Your country asked you to win a war and you did it. And that's exactly what we're being asked to do but all of a sudden our killing and getting killed is being taken out of war and turned into a battle for the ratings of prime-time television!

Have You Anything to Declare?
by Maurice Hennequin and Pierre Veber

Trivelin - 25   Male - Comic

This especially challenging monologue contains vivid narration, whimsical humor, dream, and fantasy. The character is describing an experience which plunged him from his highest hopes to deep frustration and despair; and the actor can certainly play a range of emotions along the way. The comedy must develop out of Trivelin's sincere frustration on his honeymoon.

You cannot imagine what a state I was in before the wedding. The wedding day arrived and with it the church ceremony. The breakfast, the reception. At last Paulette and I were able to disappear. We had a sleeping compartment reserved for us. We got on the train. At last we were alone. No more relatives. The train started. I took my dearest Paulette in my arms, whispering a lot of sweet, idiotic words into her ear. I kissed her little ears, first the one, then the other. Little by little she relaxed, our conversation at first was sweet, then tender, then more tender, then passionate. I was like a man possessed and she, my little darling, was beside herself. We forgot everything around us. We did not realize that the train was slowing down and coming to a halt at the border. I was in a trance, in a heavenly state of ecstasy. One moment only from my desired paradise. Suddenly the door burst open and a uniformed

35

man shouted into the compartment, "Have you anything to declare?" I couldn't carry on. I threw that uniformed monster out, but the ecstasy was gone. The heavenly state was gone. Everything was gone! I had nothing to declare!

The Bread & Roses Play, by Steve Friedman

Giovanni - 25   Male - Serious

This marvelous speech by a young immigrant to America is extremely challenging because it requires both heartfelt sincerity as well as excellent acting technique. The character has literally "found his dream" in the person of Emilia--who at present is accusing him of not loving her any longer. Thus the actor has a built-in vis-a-vis here which is possibly the strongest of any monologue in this collection. It is patched-together from several short speeches of Giovanni, so the actor should look for Emilia's reactions as the piece develops.

This is not freedom. I came here three thousand miles to be free. Not for money. Not for idleness. I am working harder with less to show than ever in my life here. But I came here for freedom! Emilia, milia, milia. I'm nothing without you. You gave me the words I'm talking with, everything. Except for you I would now be giving up in this country. All my life I have dreamed of you exactly. When I was ignorant, when I was working like a donkey loading wool on the bobbins of your machine, do you know what I lived for? To speak with you. Only enough English to speak with you, and how long it took. Because you are she. Because the first moment I saw you there was no mistake. You had in your hand a cup of water and you looked up from drinking it to see my eyes on you. But you did not look

36

away. No. But looking at me. Smiling. Not like a whore.

Like a free woman. And then you laughed. Yes. Because only

then did I arrive in America. And you were my Statue of

Liberty.

The Kid With the Big Head, by Pedro Pietri

Disabled Veteran - 20's   Male - Comic

The setting for this monologue is actually the waiting area of a
hospital emergency room where a bizarre group of low-income
people are desperately awaiting treatment. You can use this
situation to determine your choice of vis-a-vis; there are many
possibilities. But the overriding satirical tone of the piece
needs to be punctuated here and there with moments of sadness,
or nostalgia, or puzzlement in order to provide some
counterpoint and contrast in the emotional colors.

Lady, I'm a disabled veteran. I was wounded in Vietnam

defending this great country of ours so your big head son won't

have to grow up under a communist system. That might not be

your problem now but it will be your problem when your kid and

his big head get drafted into the military to fight for liberty

and justice and TV commercials. In times of national emergency

everyone goes including your kid and his big head! "Freaks to

the Front!" was the battle cry of the Vietnam conflict. They

had all kinds of abnormal military personnel ready for combat.

They had kids with big heads and kids with no heads! They had

kids that were mentally ill and kids that were terminally ill!

Our platoon sergeant used to wet the bed and suck his thumb on

dangerous search-and-destroy missions! But the most difficult

kids in Vietnam were the ones that were drafted from the

37

grave. The recently-dead and the not-so-recently-dead were exhumed and given a complete physical at the government's expense, and those that qualified and those that didn't qualify were given crewcuts, a uniform, a canteen, some bubblegum and an M-16 semi-automatic. <u>And</u> given three hours of basic training and three hours of advanced infantry training, and two hours of jungle training in an abandoned Hollywood studio, and then sent to die again for their country this time around!

<u>Mr. and Mrs. Coffee</u>, by William J. Sibley

Mauricio - 20's   Hispanic Male - Comic

<u>There is a certain nervous embarrassment combined with a disarming naivete about this character, which probably accounts for his greatest charm. The comedy is subtle here and should not be overworked but allowed to arise naturally from the honest simplicity of the character. Regard him as unfamiliar with American customs and good taste, but anxious to score a good impression.</u>

Permit me, my name is Mauricio Gomez. I am from Bogota, Colombia. I come from a very good family in Colombia. All the time I am with nice peoples. Nice peoples are very important to me. Are you going to be mean to me? All the time I am so nervous in America. When I was seven my family take me to Disneyworld. I cry every day because peoples wouldn't stop smiling at me. Everywhere we go, they are smiling . . . like this. "Why?" I ask my papa. "Why are they smiling so much?" And he say, "Because in America, the underwear fits like a glove." And then, you know, I was more nervous. "Don't be

38

nervous," that's what they tell me at Disneyworld when that damned dog "Goofy" pick me up and put me on their shoulders. You know Goofy, the big ugly dog that lives with Mickey Moose? I was to scare, I make the pee-pee in my little shorts. Goofy, he was not nice to me after that. Well, perhaps, my brother, Regelio, he is not such nice peoples. He is drug dealer, but only until he has enough money to buy the Bogota Hilton. My sister, Ophelia, already has the Sheraton. I myself have a very small Holiday Inn in Santa Marta. You must come and spend your vacation with me. We always have many nice peoples staying there. Nice peoples are very important to me.

Retro, by Megan Terry

Landy - 27   Male - Serious

Although this speech seems intolerant and even angry on its surface, the character mixes these feelings with a great deal of care and affection for his vis-a-vis. It's not that he resents what the stage offers his vis-a-vis, but more what he sees it doing to her emotionally and mentally. This offers a strong challenge for the actor to play "opposites" throughout, while at the same time sustaining a high emotional energy from beginning to end.

God you're sick. I don't want you to be in that play. I've never been more serious in my life. It's sick being in the theater. You lay your neck on the block every time you go for an audition. You're some kind of crazy masochist. How can you do that to yourself? What was all the anguish you were spouting about age a moment ago? I'm going to make you quit that phoney racket before you really go crackers on me. There's what you should be doing: writing! How long you spent on acting? How long? Yeah, fifteen years. Who are you? Kids stop you for your autograph? Is that the phone ringing with a movie contract? Just what part do you have in this "First Class" production? Do you have the first part? Are you the leading woman? Are you even the second lead? Is it even a good part? You are thirty years old. Just when are you going to be the leading woman? When? When? When?

Women of Manhattan, by John Patrick Shanley

Duke - 28   White or Black Male - Serious

Probably a good vis-a-vis for this piece is a young woman whom the character is trying to romance, a near stranger almost. This will tend to make the piece not simply an outpouring of Duke's loneliness and frustration, but also an appeal for understanding, where communication is all-important for him. The monologue's last line is especially interesting, since it permits a variety of interpretations, a few of which can suddenly reverse the mood created in the earlier sections.

If you really knew me, Judy--and I'm not sure that's possible-- but if you really could, I think you'd like me. Listen! Maybe I'm not doing a very good job, but I am trying to talk to you! This is very hard for me! I've been going from woman to woman for the last two years. I sleep with them, I get bored with them, I go on! Do you know what that's like? It's like if they dusted my body it'd be nothing but fingerprints! If they dusted my soul, well, that's when the women wore gloves. There's a bitterness in my mouth. I'm trying not to let it make me talk bitterly. To you. Because it is true what you say. I am

40

lonely. But I wonder if you know what that means. When I say I
am lonely. That is peculiar and special to me. My loneliness
is not your loneliness. Do you understand? I have this
personal world. I live in there. It's not much, but it's all I
have. I have to be sure, if I let you in, that you're not going
to wreck it! You seem very angry to me. I am angry. You're
angry. We walked in like that. I don't know what to do about
that. God, I'm so nervous. I'm sorry. I don't know what you
must think of me. I've really been having a great time.

Sunday Sermon, by David Henry Hwang

Minister - 20's   Male - Comic

The context of this outrageous monologue is a Sunday service,
and the vis-a-vis is the church congregation--a fact which
allows the actor to play the piece directly to the house.
Probably its most valuable feature for the actor is that it
should contain highly theatricalized oratorical gestures, vocal
dynamics, and rhetoric which will not seem "phoney" in the
context. Needless to say, the piece must be played with utter
seriousness and intensity, and the actor should not obviously
"work for laughs."

We thank the choir for that inspiring and enthusiastic
rendition. Today's choice of anthem seems particularly
appropriate in view of today's sermon topic. "How to Spread the
gospel in the Event of Nuclear War." I know there are people
who would rather we shy away from the tough decisions every
Christian must make once the bombs hit the ground. I do not
count myself among them. Many of us have been conditioned to
stereotype a nuclear holocaust as a bad thing. This is simply

41

narrow minded. A nuclear war can be a great tragedy or a great opportunity, a vehicle for Satan or for the soldiers of righteousness. If we don't reap the harvest of such an event, you can be sure that scores of Satan's little workers will be out sowing the seeds of evil, out amongst the maimed and wounded, enslaving them to illicit drugs, performing abortions, teaching evolution, and encouraging positive portrayals of homosexuals on our television networks. What a difference the nuclear war will make to us, the soul winners! No more houses of prostitution, no more ERA, no more drugs, no more Kurt Vonnegut! Gone will be gun-control laws, homosexual housing ordinances, busing, and teenage free clinics! And we will be able to start once again, hand-in-hand to re-create the world envisioned by the founding fathers: a nation of free men, mule and woman by their side, working the land with their hands and organizing television boycotts! When we look at it this way, is a nuclear holocaust all that bad?

Sea of Forms, by Megan Terry

Two - 20's   Male or Female - Seriocomic

This monologue is especially vividly written because it gives the actor a built-in vis-a-vis for strong communication, and an exciting situation for the character to play. This excitement, however, should not be played simply as a "news flash;" the energy must also spring from the character's own personal enthusiasm for the discovery he/she is announcing. Above all, the humorous references should be inserted deftly, like counterpoint, to the overall pace and intensity of the main narrative.

Have you heard: that the latest headline from the biology lab

is a fact of exquisite beauty? Did you know that if you allow a
scientist to extract two, only two, two out of the billions of
cells in your body, to pluck these two cells from you and place
them side by side in a pyrex dish--that these two cells without
a philharmonic orchestra--that these two cells--without a
conductor--that these two cells--without the shelter of you--
that these two cells, on their own in the wide world, will beat
together in a perfect pulse. Will pulse together in a perfect
beat. As long as they are together, outside of you on the pyrex
dish, they will beat as lovers' hearts beat. Two together, in
harmony as one. But--if you separate these cells, and place one
cell in one of your grandmother's pyrex dishes and the other in
another dish, they will beat separately. The same two cells
from the same body, they will beat on their alone and alone.

Monologues for Women

The Incredibly Famous Willy Rivers, by Stephen Metcalfe

Blonde - 20's   Female - Seriocomic

The actress must not treat this character as a stereotype but should instead look for true sincerity of feeling. The "morning after the night before" is the dramatic situation, and so a certain amount of awkwardness and uncertainty is present in the relationship between the character and her vis-a-vis. The speech also contains a strong degree of romance and fantasy beneath its everyday surface, and this should be its most charming theatrical quality in performance.

You're not like I'd thought you'd be. See, I heard they were making a movie of your life story and all, and I thought you must be sorta adventurous for them to do that. And sorta dangerous. And sorta comical in all the witty things you must all the time sorta say. And like, if you have any influence and could set up an audition. . . . Movies are great, you know? Sometimes in movies everybody is sad? Somebody has died and everybody is in mourning. Everybody is miserable and they still seem to be having a better time than I ever have. On my best days even. I thought you'd be like that. Having a better time. I'd give anything to be like you. Noticed. Most of us never get noticed for anything. I want more than that. I want . . . I want men to threaten and throw themselves off tall buildings if I won't marry them. And when I won't? They do. I'd like to feign humility while all the time accepting important awards. Thank you, everyone, thank you. I'd like to thank . . . me. I want . . . I want . . . I want. . . . I don't know what I want. It all.

<u>**The Web,** by Martha Boseing</u>

Abigail - 28   Female - Comic

<u>This piece is built on a comic contrast between a normally
conservative teacher and her outrageous sexual fantasies which
eventually emerge and take over. While starting more or less
formally as a "lecture," the actress should then develop the
speech as a footnote to the class presentation during which the
character becomes increasingly carried away by her fantasies.
The elements of mystery and secret, and near-manic enthusiasm as
the piece reaches a strong climax are very important.</u>

The interesting thing about Aristotle's theory of tragedy is its
kinship to the male orgasm. You know, I have to tell you how
pleased I am that so many of you signed up for this course. It
means a great deal to me. It's so . . . unexpected. Consider
the standard that the first four acts of a good play be built to
a slow crescendo rising up and up, at an ever-increasing
intensity of emotion, until finally the climax is reached and
there is a tremendous outburst of passion, a catharsis, if you
will, after which, in the fifth act, a speedy decrescendo
immersing the hero in an overwhelming sense of exhaustion,
expenditure and loss, until he comes to his final resting place,
usually in death. Given this classical format of biological
determinism it follows that women's plays could or should be
multiorgasmic in form, small mini-scenes perhaps, coming in
waves of emotions, crests and valleys, like the ebb and flow of
changing tides, and finally consummating in a sense of
nourishment and plenitude, the creation of new life, birth.

46

Out of our Father's House, by Eve Merriam
Paula Wagner, Jack Hofsiss

"Mother" Mary Jones - 20's   Female - Serious

Mary, as a young labor organizer in the 1800's, describes for her friends what she accomplished by a demonstration she organized in Pennsylvania.   The choice of vis-a-vis is very important because the actress must re-live the incident instead of playing it as nostalgic reminiscence.

I went to Kensington, Pennsylvania, where seventy-five thousand textile workers were on strike. Of this number, more than ten thousand were little children. They were all stooped little things, round-shouldered and skinny, some with their fingers off at the knuckles. Many of them were not yet ten years of age. I asked the newspapermen why they hadn't published the facts about child labor in Pennsylvania. They said that they couldn't because all ten mill owners had stock in the papers. "Well, I've got stock in these little children, and I'll arrange a little publicity." I decided that the children and I would go on a tour. I asked some of the parents if they'd let me have their little boys and girls for a week or ten days. I promised to bring them back safe and sound. They consented. The children carried knapsacks on their backs. They each had a knife and fork, a tin cup and a plate. One little girl had a fife, and her brother had a drum. That was our band. The children were very happy, having plenty to eat, taking baths in the streams and rivers every day. I thought, "When this strike is over and they go back to the mills, they will never have

47

another holiday like this one." We marched to Jersey City, Hoboken, Princeton and into New York. Our march was doing its work. We were bringing to the attention of the nation the crime of child labor.

Blind Desire, by Members of the Road Company Ensemble

Jean - 20's   Female - Serious

This selection is taken from a play set in an imaginary computerized future world called McMankind World. A young woman expresses her dawning awareness of the victimized role she has been taught to play all her life. The speech is a "ladder-type" which builds to a climax; but it is neatly divided halfway through so the actress can develop strong climaxes in each section, saving the major emotional power for the end.

All my life I was taught about God the Father. And I always carried an image of a grandfather-like man with the flowing beard, and whenever I would look into the sky I would see that image in my mind. I was taught that Eve was weak. When I was a child I was told to look up to my father and respect him for the distance that he kept. I was told to be nice to men because they will hire you and if you are lucky they will marry you. I was taught to compete with other women for man's attention. I was taught not to trust another woman. I was taught that blood was shameful, smelly, dirty, and not to be talked about. I was taught to be pretty and I was taught to say feminine things. I was taught that women were to be all things to all people and they weren't supposed to complain or be angry. And I saw pictures of women looking out of magazines, and they taught me that I was an actor and if I played the role I would go far. I was taught that power comes from above and not from within myself. And if I look around me, and start to see with new eyes, I begin to see that these things I was taught are not true. That I have lived a life based on facts that are not true. And I don't know what to do about it. I'm lost because all frames of reference are gone and I have no images to hold onto. And I get frightened because no one I see on the street seems to know that there is something drastically wrong. I want to grab someone by the face and scream at them that I am important. And Peg is important. And all the silent women in all the dusty corners of McMankind are important and they have their own power. And we've all been duped and we don't even know it.

Ice Dreams, by Leigh Podgorski

Rose - 27   Female - Serious

This monologue depends on the character's becoming completely caught-up in the excitement of re-living a recent past experience, and her eager desire to share it with her vis-a-vis. The actress must not overlook the storytelling quality which is propelled by the character's enthusiasm, nor the "quiet moment" which briefly punctuates the monologue towards the end, just prior to the final excited climax.

Jeez! Ya know, Laney, yesterday I was out in the garage. I was playin' some of my old stuff, and I was workin' on this. And I was gettin' really carried away. Ya know how you can get? Well, anyway, here I was all alone. And ya know how that garage echoes. Well, I'm singin', ya know, soft and quiet, and, I don't know, after a little while, it's like I'm someplace else,

I mean like another world, and I'm singin' and I'm singin', and all of a sudden I realize, I am just singin' those songs loud. I mean I was screamin' those tunes! Well when I realized it, and came back to where I was and how much noise I was makin', I just stopped--dead. My heart was poundin'! And I thought, jeez! I bet the whole darn neighborhood heard me! I just sat there, frozen, like a mouse, and it was so quiet! But I could hear all the sounds still ringin', ya know, on top of the quiet. I didn't budge. Just sat there. Listening. Then, I started to laugh, and I jumped up so quick! And I ran into the house like a crazy person! I expected the phone to be ringin' off the wall, and the cops to be poundin' on the door!

Massacre, by Leigh Podgorski

Tsashin - 20's   American Indian Female - Serious

This speech requires a wide range of emotional responses towards the situations described. The actress must also work to develop strong personal responses to the vivid imagery which alternates between brutal violence, tender compassion, incredibility, nostalgia, and other references. Pacing is all-important because the piece must not drag overmuch in its quieter moments.

My people. Savages. All my days had been spent among them. Hunting, cooking, weaving, stretching buckskin, salting meat, making moccasins and beads. In the forests, all through the mountains, all my days. Rejoicing in births, mourning for deaths. My People whose faces were not painted in violent streaks of red and blue--men and women. As my mother mounted her captives on ponies, My People, like a pack of vultures descended on the body of Nathan Meeker. They dragged it from

the office and stripped it naked and shot if full of bullet
holes. With chains they tied his hands and feet, and looping
the chains around his neck they attached them to a pony, and
pulled his body all across the compound, all through the town
until his bones were all broken, his neck snapped, and his
handsome grey head flopped to one side like a broken doll.
Savagely--oh yes, a savageness had come into my gentle People,
and it was as though they had given up their own power to the
power of the gods of war.

The Middle Ages, by A. R. Gurney, Jr.

Eleanor - 18   Female - Seriocomic

Eleanor is wrestling with an important choice for the first time
in her life. The actress must avoid a stereotype, and instead
enter into the tender and confused feelings of the character.
Eleanor is trying above all to be happy, she is honestly trying
to discover the best way of doing that. The speech contains a
strong vis-a-vis, and the situation allows for numerous
substitutions by the actor.

The party's over, Barney. Everyone's leaving. I want to leave
too. I don't want to stay here tonight, sweetie. Really, I
don't. I want my eight hours sleep. I want to go to Bermuda,
Barney. I want to lie around in the sun with Billy and the
whole gang. I want to play tennis and hear the Whiffenpoofs at
the Elbow Beach Club. What's wrong with that, Barney? What's
wrong with people having fun? I love all that, Barney. I love
all those people. They're good-looking, and they play games,
and they know all the lyrics to all the songs. You don't,
Barney. You can't sing and your tennis is terrible. You're bad

for me, Barney. Mother says so, and it's true. Every time I get with you, I get all mixed up. That's why I arranged Bermuda. You're too much for me, Barney. I don't love you, Barney. I love Billy. He was editor of the yearbook and he's going to Princeton in the fall, and he wants to be a lawyer. You? You couldn't even stay in Franklin and Marshall. What kind of a future would I have with you? I want a home. I want a family. I've never had them. I'll never get them with you, Barney. Barney? Did you hear me, Barney?

Little Victories, by Lavonne Mueller

Joan - 18   Female - Serious

This is a portrait of Joan of Arc just prior to her great victory at Orleans. The world of war, the habits of men, and the customs of the nobility are still very new to this young girl, and so she speaks feelingly about her simple values and rural background. The monologue's strength is its steady rise to a passionate, heroic climax. The actress should carefully pattern that build, develop several emotional colors along the way, and use her vis-a-vis strongly.

Let me tell you something, Captain. I don't come from a fancy family in Paris the way you do. I don't worry about low supplies of good wine, about losing my title. You know what war means to me? A mule! We had a plow mule called Belle. She was born the same day I was. Stray English soldiers would come by our farm asking for pack animals to carry their cannons and arrows. We couldn't let them have Belle. She was all we had for the fields. We'd starve. So Daddy took Belle out to the shed and cut up her legs till they were bleeding and she was limping so the enemy wouldn't take her. Belle's legs would

52

heal, we'd work her, till enemy stragglers came by, then we'd cut up Belle's legs again. We shared birthdays, Captain! And one day, after maybe the sixth time, I went to the shed where Belle was, all bleeding and lame, and I started pounding the walls. I screamed and pounded till my fists were bloody as Belle's legs. I learned something about myself that day. I learned that when I'm mad, I'm stronger than I ever knew I could be. When I'm mad, I don't feel pain. I endure. It's France that wants, Captain. Now, I have a battle to win. I'm tired and I don't have much time.

Sea of Forms, by Megan Terry and JoAnn Schmidman

Two - 20's   Female or Male - Seriocomic

This monologue is especially vividly written because it gives the actor a built-in vis-a-vis for strong communication, and an exciting situation for the character to play. This excitement, however, should not be played simply as a "news flash;" the energy must also spring from the character's own personal enthusiasm for the discovery he/she is announcing. Above all, the humorous references should be inserted deftly, like counterpoint, to the overall pace and intensity of the main narrative.

Have you heard: that the latest headline from the biology lab is a fact of exquisite beauty? Did you know that if you allow a scientist to extract two, only two, two out of the billions of cells in your body, to pluck these two cells from you and place them side by side in a pyrex dish--that these two cells without a philharmonic orchestra--that these two cells--without a conductor--that these two cells--without the shelter of you-- that these two cells, on their own in the wide world, will beat

together in a perfect pulse. Will pulse together in a perfect
beat. As long as they are together, outside of you on that
pyrex dish, they will beat as lovers' hearts beat. Two
together, in harmony as one. But--if you separate these cells,
and place one cell in one of your grandmother's pyrex dishes and
the other in another dish, they will beat separately. The same
two cells from the same body, they will beat on their own and
alone.

Stuck, by Adele Edling Shank

Margaret - 23   Female - Serious

This speech permits the actress to play strong feelings first to
her vis-a-vis and then to the audience. It's both a declaration
of her personal rights as well as a self-justification for her
ending the love affair. Though it may seem to be a speech on
women's rights, the actress must avoid a self-righteous
attitude. Instead, feelings of tenderness toward the man's
situation should alternate with her need to find happiness apart
from the relationship.

You stop that! Don't you ever talk to me that way again! I've
tried to be patient and be nice, but I'm sick and tired of your
talking as if you're the only person in the world. You're a
great big grown-up man and you asked me to have an affair with
you, remember? I was as nice to you as I could be for as long
as I could be, and if that wasn't good enough then it's your
fault, not mine. (To the audience:) I'm tired of being the bad
guy. Oh, you don't say anything, but I know you all think I
treated him mean. But you don't understand! It wasn't easy. I
tried for months, oh God! for months, to shake loose. But he
cried, and he snivelled. Oh, I got so fed up! But I didn't let

on. I mean I think he's kind of--delicate, and I really didn't want to hurt him more than I had to, but I mean really, a woman can only do so much! I did. I tried. But he was never happy, you know that? When he was with me he was always moaning about his wife. And I'll just bet you when he was with her he was moaning about me. I mean, what did he think it was going to be anyway, this affair he asked me to have, all Hollywood moonlight and no guilt? When I find a man I think is good for me I go and get him and when I think he isn't good for me anymore, it's over. And what's wrong with that?

Night Luster, by Laura Harrington

Roma - 27   Female - Serious

This tender piece offers the actor a wide range of choices for vis-a-vis, and for personal substitutions. The character is a jazz singer, but this is only of minor importance to the monologue. One of its more valuable qualities as an audition piece is that the desperation felt by the character is expressed through the form of her dream, so that emotional energy can remain strong despite the pain the character is experiencing.

I don't know. I get this feeling sometimes like I'm invisible or something. I can be standing there in a room and I'm talking and everything, and it's like my words aren't getting anywhere and I look down at myself and Jesus, sometimes my body isn't getting anywhere either. It's like I'm standing behind a one-way mirror and I can see the guys and I can hear the guys but they can't see me and they can't hear me. And I start to wonder if maybe I'm ugly or something, like maybe I'm some alien species from another planet, and I don't speak the language and I look totally weird. But I don't know this, you see, because on this other planet I had this really nice mother who told me I was beautiful and that I had a voice to die for because she loved me so much, not because it was true. And I arrive here on earth and I'm so filled with her love and her belief in me that I walk around like I'm beautiful and I sing like I have a voice to die for. And because I'm so _convinced_ and so strange and so _deluded_, people _pretend_ to listen to me . . . because they're being polite or something--or maybe they're afraid of me. And at first I don't notice because I sing with my eyes closed. But then one day I opened my eyes and I find out I'm living in this world where nobody sees me and nobody hears me. I'm just lookin' for that one guy who's gonna hear _me_, see _me_ . . . really take a chance. I mean, I hear _them_. I'm listening so hard, I hear promises when somebody's just sayin' hello. Jesus, if anybody ever heard what I've got locked up inside of me, I'd be a _star_.

Sally's Gone, She Left Her Name, by Russell Davis

Sally - 17   Female - Serious

This selection contains strong emotional colors right from the outset, and permits the actor a number of good choices for a vis-a-vis. Although the character's confusion is evident throughout the entire piece, there is a pattern of development from the particular situation at the beginning to the general at the conclusion. Above all, the actor must avoid playing too much "defeatism" in the monologue; this is the speech of a person trying to "win" understanding--not to complain about her condition.

56

Chris, everyone says corny stuff in private. In particular, me. I say things in my head, hopes, stuff like that, that sound just awful when I say them out loud. I've tried it. Doesn't sound at all like it did when I just thought it. It's the same with everybody. The same, I bet. Cause there's some kind of background music inside your head. If I say in my head, for example, I love you, Christopher, there's a background music. Otherwise how could I say it? I don't mean there's music, Chris, but something, and I can get goosebumps on my arms from thinking about you, Christopher. I can. But if I actually said to you, I love you, Christopher, immediately I would feel phoney. And you too. Cause something's awkward and we'd have to argue right away to make up and get back to normal. And I don't understand how come. How come the longer you stay in this world, the longer you see everything going on, the harder and harder it gets to say what you mean. Or why you have to keep it all in your head. The older you get the more and more stuff you have to keep in your head, all of it, never speaking, and it gets sicker and sicker inside your head until you can't hold it up anymore, and you're ashamed, and you fall over, get old, and die. I love you, Christopher, I love dad, too, Mom.

Fabiola, By Eduardo Machado

Miriam - 20's   Hispanic Female - Serious

This character is trying to adapt herself to the customs of American society, and in this speech she is questioning some of her "old country" beliefs in order to do so. It offers the actor a wide choice in her vis-a-vis, and the family situation

Wrapping grapes every New Year's Eve! "Eat a grape at midnight
and you'll be lucky!" Well, I'm living proof that it's a lie.
One year I ate twelve grapes and that year I had the mumps, the
measles, a cold for three months and Mama caught me kissing my
pillow. Why? Why do we have to do anything? It's
superstition! This whole house is full of superstition. Little
black balls wrapped around our necks. Saints with apples
underneath. Them and glasses of water. All these offerings so
Saint Barbara will do what Mama commands. Relics, icons, it's
the dark ages. Saint Barbara is not going to give Mama her
wish. She was just a spoiled princess who five hundred years
ago pretended to be a soldier, and some guy cut off her head.
And her father felt so ashamed when the town found out that his
daughter was fooling around with soldiers that he paid a pope to
make her a saint. And they all pretended that she was. And now
Mama prays to her. Hmmmm. What a joke!

Retro, by Megan Terry

Mira - 28   Hispanic Female - Serious

Listen, I got the job! They called me two hours ago! I still
can't believe it. You should have seen the competition.

58

They're getting younger every year. I was talking to this one. I swear she looked like a high school freshman. Perfect. Beautiful. She said she was twenty-two. I looked around the room and they all looked--fourteen! When I got out of there I felt--you know--that I needed to examine myself. I went to the subway, I went way down the platform and looked a long time in the gum mirror. And I said to myself, you will be thirty in six months. And you know--I can see it! for the first time I can see lines under my eyes and around my mouth. How long do you suppose they've been there? The point is I recognize something about myself. I can't tell you how beautiful the skin on that young girl was. Her cheeks were as soft and smooth as gardenia petals. Death itself couldn't have startled me so much. You know what I'm talking about, don't you? It scares me because I didn't see it coming. It makes me wonder about the inside of me. Am I less flexible in my thinking? Do I feel as much as I did? Is it real what I feel? Will I learn more as I grow older, or does the mind shrink with the skin?

Women of Manhattan, by John Patrick Shanley

Rhonda - 28   Female - Serious

Although this piece begins by developing the familiar subject of romantic rejection, it then switches midway into a discussion of loneliness and alienation. This provides a clear and strong through-line for the actress to play. However, it's also important to play the monologue as a winner--not as a loser-- which is always more dramatically engaging. Rhonda is struggling to find her place in life, she is not complaining of the bad breaks she has received.

YOU CAN'T HELP ME! How can you help me? What, you think I should go on a date and everything would be hunky dory? Sleep with some man I don't want? Maybe get pasted one to have a spiritual awakening? I don't buy it. It happens to you, okay. Try to deal with it, make sense of it. I'm not in the mood to go out and clobber the world with my idea of how it should be. This guy left me, okay? I feel like shit about it. I feel like I'm not worth thirty-five cents. Now I could run out that door and try to find somebody to plug that hole I feel in me, but I've done that before and I'm not going to do that again. I'd rather shrink down to my natural size, whatever that is, than get pumped up again. What do I need, Judy? True self-esteem. Can you give that to me? Thank you. So I'll wait. I'm not waiting for Jerry to come back. I'm not waiting to die. I'm waiting for me. And I may take awhile. I need to be alone. I've been alone all my life. I've been alone with a man beside me in my bed. I need to be truly alone now. So I can admit it. And think about it. And, I guess, so I can come up with a better invitation.

The Bread & Roses Play, by Steve Friedman

Emilia - 23   Female - Serious

This fiery monologue is filled with a range of sudden, vivid emotions. The character is desperately jealous, fighting to get her husband to return to her, and to pay her the respect she thinks he owes her. Her sudden change of mood (and tactics) at the speech's midpoint, however, must be played with all sincerity—the actress must remember that there is great love between her and her husband.

60

You think I'm blind? You think I didn't see you with mis what's-her-name, the mender? The one you were walking with when you walked through the spinning room and pretended not to see me. All the girls around me tried very hard not to laugh. Nobody wanted to look at me. My husband. And he wants to make an impression. He's a skilled worker, a weaver, and his wife is only a spinner. He's ashamed of her. I'm always hoping you'll come to the spinning room. I wait for it all day long. Listen, Giovanni, I know why you married me. I'm a citizen. Yes. So now you're a citizen too. It's all right. It's not your fault I came to this country before you. That's the circumstances. But now there has to be honor. If you don't honor me as your wife, I won't live with you. Why do you shame me? Why? You shame me behind my back and in front of my face. I don't understand this. I went to my mother. I said, Mama, I don't remember the old country. I was little when we came here. Is it different in Italy, to be married? Do the men make love to other women and the wives know about it and they don't care? She said no, it's the same as here, if the man is a good man, he's faithful. If he's not faithful, it's not right. He's not a good husband. He's a Don Giovanni. Yes, a seducer. It's like a sickness. Some men have it when they're young and they get over it. With some it only gets worse. I said, what can the wife do, when a man has this sickness? She said, pray.

61

Wait and pray. Don't laugh at me, Don Giovanni! If there isn't justice in heaven, I'll make justice right here on earth. You do what you want. But if I'm betrayed, something will happen. I'm not threatening, I'm telling you. Something will come of it.

Little Victories, by Lavonne Mueller

Susan B. Anthony - 20's   Female - Serious

This sensitive monologue reveals the inner conflict of the celebrated women's rights activist. She is speaking to a close friend, although the actress may easily select a vis-a-vis who requires more persuasive power from the character. Though the piece is mainly serious and tender in nature, the actress should not overlook opportunities for embarrassment and humor here and there.

I'm breathless . . . more than now and then. I rode a stage for ten days with a land surveyor. He reads Dickens and Shakespeare. He sketches. We laughed. Ate together. He played a little brass harmonica. He's the kind of man . . . who . . . who can sit up all night and whistle for dancing. He can make me forget everything: the rally, the vote. He reads poetry to me . . . sits close. Oh, I love a man's smell: train smoke, sweat, horses, sunshine. Sometimes I think . . . stay with him. Don't go to California. Take his warmth. Then I think of all the people who signed my petition. They depend on me. And there are the women waiting to sign my petition. And I know there's a truth stronger than the single pulse of my life!

Wetter Than Water, by Deborah Pryor

Chantel - 18   Female - Comic

This character is speaking comically about the godforsaken little island is southern Louisiana where she lives. Her vis-a-vis has just moved there. The choice of vis-a-vis, therefore, can be very flexible, and Chantel's motives for speaking the way she does can be variously interpreted. More than just comic, however, Chantel's speech is also very wacko, so this selection permits the actress to develop additional fascinating character traits. In rehearsal, the monologue should be pushed to extremes and gradually reduced from there to a level where the actress feels comfortable.

So I'm gonna teach you all about the native ways? Turn you from a tourist into a local in three easy steps? Some very important rules. One. You may have noticed the sun. It's bad news. Maybe not other places, but here it's so bright it shows you everything. And you don't want to be seeing everything. So get some extra dark glasses. Two. Gotta keep a monster gun by your bed at night. Gotta shoot 'em on sight and show 'em who's boss right away. I'm serious, Jack. Three. Stick to the road. 'Cause of all the heat and the color, you're liable to see things that ain't there and get all off your course. Things falling apart and breaking down in the tall grass. Big flowers rearing at you, poking you in the collarbone. Possums hanging upside down make faces at you, trying to get you to look at them. Don't--whatever you do. Dark glasses, monster ammo, take the straight and narrow. Simple as that. We keep scorpions for pets--this big! Sometimes, I'm lying awake in the dark and I can hear them along the floor. They keep armadillos for pets.

They have dances and it sounds like championship bowling on TV. Gotcha! Better run for help now, mister!

When the Bough Breaks, by Robert Clyman

Mary - 20's   Female - Comic

This character is an effervescent, optimistic nurse on a maternity ward. She is, of course, totally devoted to her husband, and her unquestioning acceptance of his absurd ideas lies at the heart of the comedy in this piece. The humor must not be forced, and the character must be played with all sincerity. The speech's closing remarks can be played comically or seriously, an interesting choice.

You're worrying about your little boy, aren't you? Three months early like this. You find it hard to understand why God chose you. He always does the right thing, you know. Frank, my fiance, every Saturday night he and God get into these rousing arguments. Frank says if God didn't want us to . . . you know . . . He wouldn't have built disreputable motels. Frank used to be a Jesuit, so I figure he knows what he's talking about. He says God was pretty wild Himself when He was young, so even though He has infinite wisdom when it comes to things like giving alms to the poor, He's like a reformed smoker when it comes to sex. God loves each of us, but He has a special place in His heart for preemies. Why, His own son was a preemie. Frank says God sent His son to be with us before we were ready. But if God had waited, we would have had to wait to

64

learn what perfection is. Frank thinks that preemies are God's way of teaching us about perfection. Because there's nothing else alive that's so vulnerable. And we're never closer to perfection than when we're loving something vulnerable. There's no grace in loving something strong.

Breaking the Prairie Wolf Code, by Lavonne Mueller

Esther - 28   Black Female - Serious

This is a "stepping-stone" type of monologue in which the character touches upon a number of meaningful personal family experiences in order to express her present feelings towards her absent children, the sufferings she has always endured, and her enjoyment of freedom despite the hardships she faces. It demands careful attention to pacing and energy in order that the somewhat "unconnected" reflections develop with vitality and a sense of the character's struggle. The actress must not allow the piece to drift into a style of limp reminiscence or lament.

My folks was took to the South from Africa and sold into the Fenchler family. Course the North whupped the South and they made the Constitution signed. Now I want you to know, I'm not running away to the West. I am choosing the West. Here's a pan of dough. Yesterday, I found field mice in my dough wet up for fresh bread over night. I just baked it anyway like a meat pie. My man--he yelled. He never used to wasn't like that. But he's free now. My children always had croup from the rain and nothin' to eat. Cause the Fenchler Family was stingy with their crops and we didn't eat too much. My oldest--he had to go out and lay on the grass and eat that ground like a cow eating. We lived on beans. We was hungry all day and most the night. Sometimes my Alice . . . she'd stop . . . and fan her little breasts like the flutter of a mountain bird. Just watching her cooled me. And I'd say: Alice, someday, we'll go out West. Sometimes the morning's be so nice. A breeze floating gentle with the spicy smell of pimento trees. I walking beside my little girl . . . watching her tiny feet so dainty going past all them rows of pickers. Alice is married now. With children of her own in Arkansas. I probably won't never see her. I'm in the West now. Hard as those cotton days was . . . I pine to walk beside my daughter all day long. We have a saying in Africa. "Talking with one another is loving one another." You remember that.

Hail, Mary II, by Nicholas A. Patricca

Mary - 20's   Female - Seriocomic

The "comic" aspect of this monologue is not comic in the sense of laughter or jokes, but rather the joy and optimism which the character feels because of her deeply religious and happy attitude towards all of life's problems. This is a stepping-stone form of monologue, which allows the actor to create gentle peaks and climaxes here-and-there throughout the audition, and which also allows a wide choice of vis-a-vis. The fragility and the innocence of the character are extemely challenging, and the energy in performance should not be forced.

It's an endurance test, is what it is. Each person has to figure it out for themselves. Not with their heads, Tessie, but with their hearts. People go around with their computers and their expensive machines figuring everything out. They can't figure things out like that. Like the doctors, always poking you with something, trying to get some machine to tell them something. Why don't they just ask? I'd tell them. No big

66

secret. They don't have to run people through those machines.
You see, Tessie, each person has their own box. It's not a very
big box, something like a hat box. God shakes and shakes that
box. Every day He pulls out one experience from that box. You
see, Tessie, all the experiences you're supposed to have are in
that box. It's like the grab bag at the church bazaar. He
pulls out the experience and places it very carefully in your
path. That's your experience for the day, like those vitamin
pills people take, one-a-day experiences I call them, only these
are for the soul. People get so upset. They don't understand
everything's made special for them.

A P P E N D I X A

Auditioning Tips

MECHANICAL POINTS FOR BASIC STAGING AND PREPARATION

1. Your monologues should be fully memorized and timed for the appropriate length (if there is a time limit). You do not need a plot or character explanation; the monologues should speak for themselves. The name of the character, the play's title, and the author's name should be sufficient.

2. You should not need any elaborate props or accessories. Remember that _you_ are auditioning, not your props. Always place your vis-a-vis downstage of you, and _never_ perform your audition directly to the auditors. They are there to judge your talent, not to give emotional responses to your performance.

3. Rehearse your monologues in a number of different spaces, and before different people. This will give you some experience with meeting stage fright and with encountering a strange audition space. Learn to create whatever "environment" you need strictly from your imagination.

4. Prepare a verbal resume, if you are auditioning for a play. Be prepared for the typical questions: "Tell me a little about yourself." or "Tell me about the work you've been doing." Speak enthusiastically but honestly about the positive things in your background, and remember that this is also part of the audition.

5. Your audition begins the moment you leave your seat or pass the curtain and come into view of the auditors. They are evaluating things about you from the first moments that they see you. You are auditioning until you have completely left the stage and are out of sight.

6. Practice your monologues several different ways in order to avoid "locking yourself" into any set pattern which may deaden your playing and lead to a mechanical performance. This is a good way to "stay fresh" with any frequently-used material. Having two or three other monologues prepared can also be helpful in keeping your imagination fresh with any given piece you may choose to play.

7. Be prepared for long delays when auditioning. Devise your own methods for keeping your mind alert while waiting, and avoid letting your energy drain-off, your attitude to become negative, or your concentration to drift into worry-thoughts.

8. _Always_ warm up immediately prior to the audition. Running-over the words of your audition in your head is useless.

Find a corner or a space to speak the monologue and to physicalize. If possible, arrive at the audition site early enough to examine the performance area and test the acoustics.

9. Remember that at every audition, <u>you</u> are the other "character" who is auditioning as you announce your name and describe your monologue in the introduction. Practice this part of the audition, too, so that the auditors learn a few important things about you just from the way you present yourself onstage.

10. <u>Never</u> begin again if you feel you've messed the monologue up somehow. Never direct any questions at the auditors unless they invite you to do so.

11. Pay attention to your appearance. Hair should be neat but natural. Clothes should look nice and also be appropriate to the characters you're portraying. Remember this is not a job interview, neither is it a McDonald's counter. You should look your best in clothes that are appropriate to the parts you're auditioning for. Your clothes are a costume too. They should be loose-fitting and not inhibit your movement or acting in any way.

12. Do not <u>ever</u> take more than one or two seconds to "get into character." Do your best piece first. Keep your volume up, and relate to the audience as a group. Don't ignore them.

<u>PSYCHOLOGICAL FACTORS FOR PREPARATION AND PERFORMANCE</u>.

<u>The following comments have been taken from actors, directors, writers, and others in a variety of contexts, all of which relate to the subject of auditioning. While some refer to technical points of an audition performance, others deal with the problems of attitude, or energy. All are important to bear in mind</u>.

"I don't choose the people, the people choose themselves. When they stand up there and you see their eyes, their demeanor, and the way they hold their head, you pretty well know it when a person belongs. Although we finally select them, they do a great deal to help us make that choice."

--Jay Blackton,Casting Director

"It's not just what they do in the piece that's important. But from the moment they walk into the room until they leave--that's

70

what affects you in terms of whether you remember them or not."

                    --Harold Baldridge, Director

"There's a certain chemistry to an actor when he walks onstage. He alters the state of the stage, he has the potential to make everything shift."

                    --Michael Leibert, Director

"The purpose of performing is to derive pleasure for yourself as well as give the best you can to the public, the best of what the piece is about. It's a hell of a lot of energy one musters out of emotions, physically and intellectually, emotionally. The point is to do well for yourself. I mean, if you don't derive any pleasure from it, forget it."

                    --Maria Ewing, Actress

"I think that the most you can expect as an actor from that prepared monologue--you're not going to get a job from that monologue. I don't know any actor who's gotten a job from a monologue--is a chance to read for the part. So the more you can show me in two minutres of who you are, the more I can get an instinctive feeling about whether I'd like to spend three weeks working intensely with you."

                    --Cathy Goedert, Casting Director

"Before I go out on an audition I tell myself I have to give one-hundred percent; if I don't, there are two million other people out there who will!"

                    --Valerie Landsburg, Actress

"You look very much for the swiftness of attack, and the swiftness of feeling, the swiftness of body movements--energy, energy, particularly energy. Where is the energy: Vocal? Emotional? Intellectual? I want some kind of body that really has energy because it takes tremendous energy to do a play. Most young actors don't have any idea of how much energy it takes. That's the biggest difference between a pro and a college student. Almost always. The young actor may have a lot of physical strength, but he or she doesn't know how to focus it."

                    --Bob Goldsby, Director

"A good audition never goes unnoticed. It may not achieve immediate employment, but no director, casting agent, or composer/lyricist ever forgets first-rate work. There is just too little of it."

--David Craig, Coach

"I first check to see that they have a very specific situation in their mind that leads them to very specifically visualizing and personalizing who it is they're talking to and what it is they want from that person. Why is it that they need to--that they can't not, make a speech to this person?"

--Alan Fletcher, Director

"I don't make people try and see their vis-a-vis, I think that's silly. There's nobody there and we all know there's nobody there. It's the way in which they inform the relationship that creates whether there's somebody there anyway. I see in monologues that often their vis-a-vis agrees with them, or is a good listener. So they give lip service to that vis-a-vis but never really deal with the person, never make contact. Using an opposite vis-a-vis for the monologue is probably the best exercise we have."

--Jane Brody, Actress/Coach

"When you're working-up an audition always keep one thing in mind: 'Would you ask people to pay money to see that?'"

--Aaron Frankel, Director

"You have to develop the monologue, structure it, orchestrate it. It must have a beginning, a middle, and an end. Don't under any circumstances, let the character be at the end where he was at the start. In an audition, honesty and truthfulness just aren't enough. The piece must have strength and variety, and it's got to go somewhere. When you're auditioning, you have only a few minutes to show them what you can do, to reveal that you have a whole spectrum of brilliant colors on your palette and not just one nice little pastel."

--Sydney Walker, Actor/Coach

"We want to see the actor's magic. It is the actor we are listening to, not the character on the pages--but there must be some connection to the character as the actor sees him on those too few pages. The connection evolves out of the choices the actor makes. The actor might fall flat on his face but he must be willing and able to take chances."

--Ginger Friedman, Casting Director

I try to serve the play in casting, but I also think, "Do I want to spend the next three months with these people? Are they going to bring something to the rehearsals? Do they love the play?" That's crucial. The actor's love of the play comes across the footlights. Doing the play merely as a job also communicates itself to the audience. An actor who is perhaps slightly less skilled but who has an astounding love for the work is the one I'll always cast.

--Gregory Mosher, Director

I allow a tremendous amount of freedom. I know what I want from the beginning and I try to shape the performance. But I want the actors to bring their own ideas, their own business, to their roles. The kind of actor I like to work with experiments constantly. The work of such actors inspires me and inspires the other actors.

--Carole Rothman, Director

I do have something in mind for each role, but I always expect the actor is going to make a major contribution. I give the actor full opportunity to create within my boundaries. If an actor doesn't at some point, in some way, surprise me by his character revelations, I'm disappointed.

--Lloyd Richards, Director

INSPIRATIONAL POINTS WHICH LIE BEHIND AUDITIONING

"You've got to like those people, I think, and you've got to like what you're doing. If you have any doubts, then-get out! I really think get out because nobody wants to see somebody who is not committed. I don't want to see a doctor who is not committed, I don't want to see a teacher who is not committed. I don't want to see anybody just passing time."

--Karen Morrow, Actress

"The best thing to do about auditioning is to form your own company so you won't have to audition any more."

--Joan Schirle, Actress/Producer

"Exciting people are committed people, in art, in politics, or in life. And it is to your advantage to be exciting. So be dedicated; it will offend the weak, but it will inspire others. A life of dedication (to your art, hopefully, but even to yourself) is fulfilling: it galvanizes your talents and directs your energies. It characterizes all great artists of all times."

--Robert Cohen, Director/Coach

"In good plays--certainly in great plays--characters don't have conversations; they have "confrontations." People don't "meet" in good plays or great plays; they have "encounters." Only in life or on television drama do people have conversations and meetings. <u>Meetings</u> and <u>conversations</u> connote something civilized and there's nothing civilized about good drama, drama that plays upon a stage and that resonates beyond what it seems to be. Drama is messy, unsubtle, often gross and always explosive."

--Frank Gagliano, Actor

"You have to really want to do it. It just means more to you than most things in life, being up there onstage, or being part of theatre, whatever it is. And stick with it when it gets bad."

--Monte Davis, Actor

"If it's a happy life you want, and if there's anything you'd like to do besides this, go do it."

--Ned Schmidtke, Coach

"Well, the only thing you can say to a young actor of any kind is this: if they want to be actors, then they just stay on it. They persist, and they take lessons and they study and they live it and they work it. You've got to act every day. Get a tape recorder, read things, listen to yourself, go to little theatres, join little theatres. That's the thing you've got to do, you've got to work at it. That's the only way, really."

--Joseph Barbera, Producer

"The key is to bring in a little love. You know, you bring a little love for the work. If you really love the work, it shows. And if you want to transmit that work, transmit that love to those who may be watching, including the audience, your primary concern would be to give them something, rather than to evaluate what you are going to be back. And that's the key, I think. Whether they like you or don't like you is irrelevant.

It's how much you liked them"

--Darryl Hickman, Producer

"Auditions are always rough. They get easier. Just don't try
to impress anyone. Just go there and do what you know you can
do, as honestly as you can do it. And whatever quality they are
looking for may not be the quality you might show at that
moment. It's not a personal thing. It's just that the director
wants an element which he did not see in you at that moment, and
you have to remember that."

--Ruth Schudson, Actress

"I am a disciplined and well trained actor. I can wrap ten
meanings around one word in two seconds. That's not boasting,
it's just flagrant, baroque, useless talent. Why do I have to
show off how technically proficient I am? I have a passionate
vision, but it's there to express and not to manipulate. That's
why I call myself an actor."

--John Hurt, Actor

"You do the best that you can do at that given time with what
you have to work with. You go in, you do your job, you shake
the hands and you say goodbye and you close the door. And this
is something I've found helps a lot. Leave it there. Don't
take the audition home with you. Let it go. Forget about it.
Maybe you will get the job, and if you do, that's great. But if
you don't, then you don't. There'll be other things. Don't
beat yourself up. It's really not worth it.

--Stepfanie Kramer, Actress

The greatest acting is simple.

--Linda Hunt, Actress

I think being out of work affects people's acting. I think a
lot of the tension you see on the stage in New York comes from
people who are frustrated about their careers. There is an aura
of desperation. If you've been out of work for awhile, each
audition gets successively worse, less carefree and easy. For
an actor, ease on the stage--to be able to approach material
without showing effort, to be relaxed, though not facile--is a
very important quality.

--Robert Joy, Actor

I always look for intelligent actors. It's easier to

communicate. The brighter the actor, the more he brings. If I
can't visualize the actor in the part during an audition, I
probably can't get it to work on the stage.

--Melvin Bernhardt, Director

I want to do a role when I feel a connection with the writing.
It's a chemical thing, the same way as when you're attracted to
another person. I don't know why it happens sometimes and why
it doesn't happen other times. Somehow, it's a kind of music I
hear or don't hear.

--Tom Hulce, Actor

The interesting thing to me is showing a person's life in
transition, the changes. That's always something I look for--
what is the progress? Certainly a character who has his life
changed, or who chooses to change, is the most interesting.
This is what an actor does: illuminate the human condition in
some way. "I see" is the ideal reaction from an audience.

--Donald Moffat, Actor

I do all the homework I can so that the day the camera starts
rolling I'm in a totally spontaneous state of mind and I stay
out of the character's way and let him take over. If you've
done your homework you let your character take you through it.
I think the preparation of a character is as rewarding as the
doing of it. They can't take the creative process away from me
if they cut a scene of mine. The preparation of a character is
what I get off on. The other stuff is like gravy.

--Andy Garcia, Actor

APPENDIX B

Resource Materials for Young Actors

A. ANTHOLOGIES OF MONOLOGUES AND SCENES

Bard, Messaline, Newhouse, eds. "And What Are You Going to Do for Us?" Toronto: Simon & Pierre, 1987. Individual speeches from more than forty of Canada's award-winning plays. Synopses on authors, production dates, and rehearsal suggestions.

Bell, Richard O., and Kuder, Joan. Auditions and Scenes from Shakespeare. Boulder, Colo: Armado and Moth, 1984. A 175-page directory of 700 selections from the entire Shakespearean dramatic canon. Each directory listing provides the number of male-female actors, approximate time length, suggestions for editing, and play or situation synopses.

Earley, Michael and Keil, Philippa. Soliloquy! The Shakespeare Monologues. 2 Vols. New York: Applause, 1986. These two volumes (for men and women, respectively) contain over 175 pieces drawn from all the 37 Shakespearean plays. Each selection has its own reference notes, and a brief introduction provides helpful hints on acting Shakespeare.

_____. Solo! The Best Monologues of the 80's. 2 Vols. New York: Applause, 1987. There are over 150 speeches in these volumes, which have been fairly carefully selected with actors' needs in mind. Each selection contains notes on character, context, and approach. Limited exclusively to plays from the 1980's (as the title implies), with separate volumes for men and women.

_____. Classic American Monologues. 2 Vols. New York: Applause, 1987. These volumes contain the most memorable speeches from American writers. More helpful as a class text than an auditions reference, however, since many of the selections are "signature pieces" (done by famous stage and screen actors) or frequently performed for auditions situations. An introductory section provides the actor with a brief overview of American theatre history. The selections include notes on character and context.

Grumbach, Jane, and Emerson, Robert. Actor's Guide to Monologues. 2 Vols. New York: Drama Book Specialists, 1974.

_____. Monologues: Men,
2 Vols. New York: Drama Book Specialists, 1976.

_____. Monologues:
Women, 2 Vols. New York: Drama Book Specialists,
1976. These four paperbacks contain actual pieces, all
drawn from contemporary British and American plays.
Many of the selections tend to be good, although most
are really only suitable for class work. The publisher
updates this collection every few years, the monologues
are almost all taken from commercially-available
scripts and New York successes. It's probably the most
commonly-used anthology for auditionees.

Handman, Wynn. Modern American Scenes for Student Actors.
New York: Bantam, 1978. All the selections are
contemporary up to the publication date, but the book
is really suitable only for classwork since its
material is so dated. It does contain some very good
monologues in addition to the scenes, but the
monologues have been frequently used over the years.

Price, Jonathan. Classic Scenes. New York: Mentor,
1979. Don't let the date deter you because the
classics are timeless. This is a must for many types
of conservatory auditions, scholarship competitions,
and any audition which requires classical material.
Although it is widely used as a scene-study text in
acting classes since it is scenes and not monologues,
most of the selections contain long passages from which
audition extracts can be easily taken.

Keil, Carl. Soliloquy! The Elizabethan and Jacobean
Monologues. 2 Vols. New York: Applause, 1987. Over
fifty speeches of all types from this theatrical
period, each edited for the actor, with helpful notes
and an introduction about acting verse drama. Separate
volumes for men and women.

Reay, Corey, Caught in the Act. Toronto: Simon & Pierre,
1987. Forty comic characters created by Corey around
the theme of contemporary mores. Original, witty, and
often irreverent.

Rudnicki, Stefan. Classical Monologues, 4 Vols. New
York: Drama Book Specialists, 1979-82. These
paperbacks are strictly for auditions requiring
classical material. They are more limited than the
collection by Jonathan Price just listed, because
Rudnicki concerns himself almost exclusively with

Renaissance authors.

Schewel, Amy, and Smith, Marisa. <u>The Actor's Book of Movie Monologues</u>. New York: Viking-Penguin, 1986. This is a fun book with much infrequently-done material. Young actors should be careful on two counts, however: not many of the selections fall within the age range of young performers, and many of the selections are "signature" pieces which famous screen actors have made very familiar.

Schulman, Michael, and Mekler, Eva. <u>Contemporary Scenes for Student Actors</u>. New York: Penguin, 1980. This paperback contains only scenes, but the first fourteen pages present one of the most valuable approaches to scene acting that can be found anywhere.

Seto, Judith R. <u>The Young Actor's Workbook</u>. New York: Grove, 1984. An excellent up-to-date book containing fifty scenes and monologues with character descriptions, plot synopses, and explanations of settings. For classwork and auditions possibilities.

Steffenson, James L., Jr. <u>Great Scenes from the World Theater</u>. New York: Avon, 1971. Once again, don't let the date scare you off because it's an absolute <u>must</u> for any auditions requiring classical material. Like Jonathan Price's book mentioned above, the scenes often contain extended speeches which can be used for auditioning.

B. **<u>HANDBOOKS ON AUDITIONING TECHNIQUES</u>**

Acker, Iris Y. <u>The Secret of How to Audition for Commercials</u>. Miami, Fla.: I.Y.A. Publishing, 1980. Excellent nuts and bolts approach to the business and the technique of acting in this challenging medium. Contains a number of sample commercials for practice and helpful "tip sheets."

Craig, David. <u>On Singing Onstage</u>. New York: Macmillan, 1978. The classic text for preparing theatrical songs. Don't try to rehearse for a singing audition without it. Excellent text for experienced singers as well as very useful for actors without much formal training.

Ellis, Roger. <u>A Student Actor's Audition Handbook</u>. Chicago: Nelson-Hall, 1985. The most up to date basic text for stage and musical auditioning. Also contains valuable chapters on resumes, interviews, musical theatre auditions, and numerous exercises for class or solo work. Written specifically for the young, actor.

Finchlevy, Joan. Audition! A Complete Guide for Actors, with an Annotated Selection of Readings. New York: Prentice-Hall, 1984. Contains the most recent listings of play selections through the publication date, as well as helpful suggestions for preparing the audition.

Fridell, Squire. Acting in Television Commercials for Fun and Profit. New York: Crown 1980. Don't be put-off by this simplistic title. The book will definitely satisfy any curiosity you may have about this critical and lucrative sector of the industry.

Hunt, Gordon. How to Audition. New York: Harper and Row, 1977. Although somewhat dated now, it contains numerous comments from working professionals on the auditions process, as well as a number of helpful guidelines for preparing auditions. Good reading for young actors, although many of the acting methods are more suitable for experienced professionals.

Shurtleff, Michael, Audition. New York: Walker, 1980. A book for professionals on the "Shurtleff approach" to auditions and stage acting. This is the most widely-used audition book on the market, although it is difficult for beginning students to use it alone, without workshop instruction by a Shurtleff-trained instructor.

Silver, Fred. Auditioning for the Musical Theatre. New York: New Market, 1985. An easy-to-read guide for preparing your musical auditions, this is the actor's "Bible" for training yourself in performing good musical theatre auditions.

C. BOOKS ON THE ACTING PROFESSION

Cohen, Robert. Acting Professionally. 3rd ed. Palo Alto: Mayfield, 1981. The most straightforward, accurate, and honest description of the business of being an actor, by a working professional. "Must" reading for every would-be young actor.

Hunt, Cecily. How to Make Money and Get Started in Commercials and Modelling. New York: Van Nostrand Rinehart, 1982. As its title suggests, this is an excellent book for breaking into the commercial aspects of the industry without much experience. It is filled with detail, necessary facts, up-to-date information and exercises.

Katz, Judith. The Business of Show Business. New York: Harper and Row, 1981. A highly motivational and very readable book, it lays out the many options open to young actors--and it does it in a way that takes the dreadful "mystique" out of the profession to make it much more understandable.

Logan, Tom. How to Act and Eat at the Same Time. Washington, D.C.: Communications Press, 1982. Like the Cohen book, an indispensable manual for breaking-in. Up-to-date figures and good information, but no treatment of acting methods for preparing audition material.

_____. Acting in the Million Dollar Minute: the Art and Business of Performing in TV Commercials. Washington, D.C.: Communications Press, 1984. Like his other book, this one is also detailed and indispensable for anyone considering this aspect of the profession.

Lydon, Michael. How to Succeed in Show Business by Really Trying. New York: Dodd, Mead, 1985. Another good nuts and bolts primer for breaking into the acting business. This one stresses the value of personal initiative and hard work as means for getting your career to pay off.

Markus, Tom. The Professional Actor. New York: Drama Book Specialists, 1979. An excellent book for student actors. Surveys the whole field of acting and outlines the best methods for selling oneself eventually in the professional marketplace. Highly readable, composed with the young actor in mind.

McNoughton, Robert, and McNoughton, Bruce. Act Now: An Actor's Guide for Breaking-In. Hollywood: Global, 1982. An outstanding up-to-date perspective on stage and film acting, dealing especially with young actors. Emphasizes how an acting career is a very realistic choice, and describes several avenues for young actors to follow.

Moore, Dick. Opportunities in Acting Careers. Lincolnwood, Ill.: National Textbook Co., 1986. A very thorough glimpse into the process of building an acting career. Written especially for undergraduate and graduate university students.

Rogers, Lynne, and Henry, Marie. How to Be a Working Actor. New York: Evans, 1986. Step-by-step procedures for getting yourself established today. Up to date, with a very business like approach to marketing oneself, from two women who learned it from the ground up.

CREDITS

10036.

<u>The Grunt Childe</u> is reprinted by permission of the author, and was originally produced by Artistic Director Mako and East West Players in Los Angeles, California.

<u>Retro</u> and <u>Sea of Forms</u> by Megan Terry are reprinted by permission of the author. For all performances and/or reprint rights turn to Elisabeth Marton, 96 Fifth Avenue, New York, New York 10011.

<u>Los Vendidos</u> by Luis M. Valdez is reprinted by permission of the author, and by the Writers and Artists Agency, 11726 San Vicente Boulevard, Suite 300, Los Angeles, California 90049.

<u>Fabiola</u> is reprinted by permission of the author, Eduardo Machado, 799 Broadway #325, New York, New York 10003.

<u>The Middle Ages</u>, ©1978, by A.R. Gurney, Jr., ©1976, by A.R. Gurney, Jr. as an unpublished dramatic composition. ALL RIGHTS RESERVED. CAUTION: Professionals and amateurs are hereby warned that THE MIDDLE AGES is subject to a royalty. It is fully protected under the copyright laws of the United States of America, and of all countries covered by the International Copyright Union (including the Dominion of Canada and the rest of the British commonwealth), and of all countries covered by the Pan-American Copyright Convention, and of all countries with which the United States has reciprocal copyright relations. All rights, including professional, amateur, motion picture, recitation, lecturing, public reading, radio broadcasting, television, and the rights of translation into foreign languages are strictly reserved. Particular emphasis is laid on the question of readings, permission for which must be secured from the author's agent in writing. All inquiries (except for stock and amateur rights) should be addressed to Gilbert Parker, William Morris Agency, Inc., 1350 Avenue of the Americas, New York, New York 10019. The stock and amateur production rights in THE MIDDLE AGES are controlled exclusively by the Dramatists Play Service, Inc., 440 Park Avenue South, New York, New York 10016. No stock or amateur performance of the play may be given without obtaining in advance the written permission of the Dramatists Play Service, Inc., and paying the requisite fee. <u>The Middle Ages</u>, was produced upon the New York stage by Stephen Graham.

<u>Have You Anything to Declare</u> is used by permission of the authors, Maurice Hennequin and Pierre Veber, translated and adapted by Robert Cogo-Fawcett and Braham Murray. All questions concerning reprint or performance rights should be addressed to the authors' agent, Felix DeWolfe, 1 Robert Street, Adelphi,

85